CAMBRIDGE LIBRARY COLLECTION

Books of enduring scholarly value

Slavery and Abolition

The books reissued in this series include accounts of historical events and movements by eye-witnesses and contemporaries, as well as landmark studies that assembled significant source materials or developed new historiographical methods. The series includes work in social, political and military history on a wide range of periods and regions, giving modern scholars ready access to influential publications of the past.

A Representation of the Injustice and Dangerous Tendency of Tolerating Slavery

This work by the anti-slavery campaigner Granville Sharp (1735–1813) brings together legal and historical documents, as well as the author's own legal arguments, demonstrating that slavery was illegal and therefore could not be upheld in England. Furthering his own intellectual development while working for a linen draper, Sharp later became a government clerk and pursued a writing career. His awakening to the horrors of the slave trade resulted from a chance encounter with an injured slave seeking help from his physician brother. Carrying out the necessary legal research, Sharp published this book in 1769 to demonstrate that slavery has no basis in English law. In 1772, the landmark case of James Somerset was brought before Lord Mansfield, who upheld Sharp's contention: as a result, it was henceforth understood that any slave reaching the shores of England became free. Sharp's memoirs of his life are also reissued in this series.

Cambridge University Press has long been a pioneer in the reissuing of out-of-print titles from its own backlist, producing digital reprints of books that are still sought after by scholars and students but could not be reprinted economically using traditional technology. The Cambridge Library Collection extends this activity to a wider range of books which are still of importance to researchers and professionals, either for the source material they contain, or as landmarks in the history of their academic discipline.

Drawing from the world-renowned collections in the Cambridge University Library and other partner libraries, and guided by the advice of experts in each subject area, Cambridge University Press is using state-of-the-art scanning machines in its own Printing House to capture the content of each book selected for inclusion. The files are processed to give a consistently clear, crisp image, and the books finished to the high quality standard for which the Press is recognised around the world. The latest print-on-demand technology ensures that the books will remain available indefinitely, and that orders for single or multiple copies can quickly be supplied.

The Cambridge Library Collection brings back to life books of enduring scholarly value (including out-of-copyright works originally issued by other publishers) across a wide range of disciplines in the humanities and social sciences and in science and technology.

A Representation of the Injustice and Dangerous Tendency of Tolerating Slavery

Granville Sharp

CAMBRIDGE
UNIVERSITY PRESS

University Printing House, Cambridge, CB2 8BS, United Kingdom

Cambridge University Press is part of the University of Cambridge.
It furthers the University's mission by disseminating knowledge in the pursuit of education, learning and research at the highest international levels of excellence.

www.cambridge.org
Information on this title: www.cambridge.org/9781108075657

This edition first published 1769
This digitally printed version 2014

ISBN 978-1-108-07565-7 Paperback

A REPRESENTATION OF THE INJUSTICE AND DANGEROUS TENDENCY OF TOLERATING SLAVERY IN ENGLAND.

A
REPRESENTATION
OF THE
Injuſtice and Dangerous Tendency
O F
TOLERATING SLAVERY;
OR OF
ADMITTING THE LEAST CLAIM
O F
Private Property in the Perſons of Men, in England.

IN FOUR PARTS.

CONTAINING,

I. Remarks on an Opinion given in the Year 1729, by the (then) Attorney General and Sollicitor General, concerning the Caſe of Slaves in Great Britain.

II. The Anſwer to an Objection, which has been made to the foregoing Remarks.

III. An Examination of the Advantages and Diſadvantages of tolerating Slavery in England. The latter are illuſtrated by ſome Remarks on the Spirit of the Plantation Laws, occaſionally introduced in Notes, which demonſtrate the cruel Oppreſſion, not only of Slaves, but of Free Negroes, Mulattoes, and Indians, and even of Chriſtian White Servants in the Britiſh Colonies.

IV. Some Remarks on the ancient Villenage, ſhewing, that the obſolete Laws and Cuſtoms, which favoured that horrid Oppreſſion, cannot juſtify the Admiſſion of the modern Weſt Indian Slavery into this Kingdom, nor the leaſt Claim of Property, or Right of Service, deducible therefrom.

BY GRANVILLE SHARP.

L O N D O N:

PRINTED FOR BENJAMIN WHITE, (NO. 63) IN FLEET-STREET, AND ROBERT HORSFIELD, (NO. 22) IN LUDGATE-STREET.

M DCC LXIX.

A

REPRESENTATION, &c.

PART I.

Remarks on an opinion given in the year 1729, *by the (then) Attorney and Solicitor General, concerning Slaves brought to Great Britain.*

PREAMBLE TO THE OPINION*.

" IN order to certify a miſtake, that " Slaves become free by their being in

* This is copied from a MS. collection of opinions, caſes, &c. in the hands of a gentleman of the law: but the opinion, without the preamble, may be ſeen in the XIth volume of the Gentleman's Magazine.

 Eng-

" England, or being baptized, it hath
" been thought proper to consult the King's
" Attorney and Solicitor General in Eng-
" land thereupon; who have given the fol-
" lowing opinion, subscribed with their
" own hands."

OPINION.

" We are of opinion, that a Slave by
" coming from the West-Indies to Great-
" Britain, or Ireland, either with or with-
" out his master, doth not become free;
" and that his master's property or right
" in him, is not thereby determined or
" varied; and that baptism doth not bestow
" freedom on him, nor make any altera-
" tion in his temporal condition in these
" kingdoms: We are also of opinion, that
" the master may legally compel him to
" return again to the plantations."

P. YORK.
C. TALBOT.

Jan. 14, 1729.

The authority of these great names is such, that I might seem guilty of an unpardonable presumption, if I should com-

 mence

mence my criticiſm on this opinion by any other method, than that of comparing it with the ſentiments of other perſons, who have conſidered the ſame ſubject.

" It is ſaid, that the law of England is " favourable to liberty; and ſo far this " obſervation is juſt, that when we had " men in a ſervile condition amongſt us, " the law took advantage even of neglects " of the maſters to enfranchiſe the villain, " and ſeemed for that purpoſe even to ſub- " tilize a little; becauſe our anceſtors " judged, that *freemen were the real ſupport* " *of the kingdom.*" (See the Account of the European Settlements in America, vol. ii. part vi. ch. xii. p. 130.) Another remark of the ſame ingenious author (in p. 118.) conveys a very ſenſible idea of thoſe juſt and equitable reaſons, which probably induced our anceſtors to render the Engliſh laws ſo indulgent to the oppreſſed villain.

" Indubitably" (ſays he) " the ſecurity, " as well as the ſolid wealth of every na- " tion, conſiſts principally in the number " of low and middling men of a free con- " dition, and that beautiful gradation from " the higheſt to the loweſt, where the " tranſitions all the way are almoſt im-

" perceptible.—To produce this, ought to " be the aim and mark of every well regu- " lated common-wealth, and *none has ever* " *flourished upon other principles.*"

The vassalage of Scotland was considered by our legislature, as highly injurious to the welfare of that kingdom, dangerous to this, and unjust in itself: it was therefore abolished by an Act * of Parliament in the twentieth year of King George

* This Act (according to the preamble) is " for ex- " tending the *influence*, *benefit* and *protection* of the " King's *laws* and *courts of justice* to *all his Majesty's* " *subjects in Scotland*;" yet it must be confessed, that *some of* his Majesty's subjects in Scotland, (viz. those who work in the collieries, saltworks, or mines) seem still to be exposed in too great a degree to the will of their employers, by the 21st section; unless it should be allowed, that the clause is expressed in such terms, that it cannot justify any arbitrary proceedings.

And indeed, there is some room for a favourable interpretation, the proprietor being only at liberty to exercise " *such power and authority as is competent to him by* " *law.*"

Therefore, as the law cannot authorize an unjust oppression, the above-mentioned "*power and jurisdiction,*" may (I hope) be considered as a mere shadow of vassalage, without effect.

Nevertheless there will not be wanting interested persons to urge, that the clause is sufficiently effectual, and that it must necessarily be understood to imply and authorize a continuation of the former vassalage, over " *all workmen employed in carrying on coalworks, salt-* " *works, and mines in Scotland.*" But even if this should really be true, I will venture one objection against it, viz. that the same is absolutely unnecessary, if not hurt-

 ful

the ſecond, (A. D. 1747. ch. xliii. " An " Act for taking away and aboliſhing the " Heretable Juriſdictions in that Part of " Great-Britain called Scotland, &c.") for which ſalutary meaſure, all true friends to the liberty of Great Britain ought to be thankful.

Indeed there are many inſtances of perſons being freed from Slavery by the laws of England; but (God be thanked) there is neither law, nor even a precedent (at leaſt I have not been able to find one) of a legal determination, to juſtify a maſter in claiming or detaining any perſon whatſoever as a Slave in England, who has not voluntarily bound himſelf as ſuch by a contract in writing.

In the caſe of Gallway verſus Caddee, tried before Baron Thompſon at Guildhall, about 30 years ago *, verdict was given for the defendant, in behalf of a Negro claimed by the plaintiff as his Slave, whom the

ful to the true intereſt of the proprietors of ſuch works. The learned Baron Monteſquieu clearly demonſtrates this point, (viz. " Inutilité de L'Eſclavage parmi nous.") in the 8th chap. of his 15th book, des L'Eſprit de Loix. See further remarks on this head in the IVth part.

* The author accidentally met with a gentleman who was preſent at this trial.

court declared to be *free on his firſt ſetting foot on Engliſh ground.*

Alſo in the caſe of De Pinna, &c. verſus Henriques, (who protected a poor Negro woman, claimed by the plaintiffs as their Slave) a verdict was given for the defendant at Guildhall in 1732.

Lord Chief Juſtice Holt held, that "as "ſoon as a Negro comes into England, he "becomes free: one may be a villain in "England, but not a Slave." See Salkeld's Reports, vol. ii. p. 666.

"Slaves may claim their freedom as ſoon "as they come into England, Germany, "France, &c." Groenwig Vinnius adht. Wood's Civ. Inſt. b. i. ch. ii. p. 114.

The ſtate of Slaves amongſt the ancient Romans or other heathen nations, and the imaginary right of conquerors in thoſe early days to enſlave their captives, do not at all concern a Chriſtian government; ſo that it would be ſuperfluous to quote the learned Grotius's conſiderations on theſe ſubjects; becauſe ſuch precedents cannot be of any authority amongſt Chriſtians. 'Tis ſufficient for our purpoſe, that theſe heathen cuſtoms are not now eſtabliſhed in Europe, and that even Grotius himſelf allows the ſame.

After

After ſpeaking of the aſylum given by the Jews to Slaves, who had fallen into that unhappy ſtate, without any fault of their own, he obſerves as follows: "Quali "ex cauſa videri poteſt ortum jus *quod in* "*ſolo Francorum ſervis datur proclamandi in* "*libertatem, quanquam id nec quidem nunc* "*tantum bello captis ſed & aliis qualibuſlibet* "*ſervis videmus dari.*" Grotius, lib. iii. cap. vii. ſect. viii. p. 735. Gronovius further explains theſe words, ("Servis datur "proclamandi,") in the following note, viz. "*Ut Servus peregrinus, ſimul atque ter-* "*ram Francorum tetigerit, eodem momento* "*liber fiat.*" * Gronovius.

I may add farther, that it is, and ever has been, the conſtant practice of Juſtices of the Peace in England, (if I except a certain mercenary trading Juſtice at the Weſt end of the town) to enlarge all perſons who demand the Magiſtrate's protection from the tyranny of Slaveholders. Therefore it muſt appear, that Slavery is by no means tolerated in this iſland, either by the law or cuſtom of England; though

* "That a foreign Slave, as ſoon as he ſhall have "touched European ground, the ſame moment may be "made free."

the opinion, which I now propoſe to examine, inculcates a very different doctrine: but, indeed, it is expreſſed in ſuch *general* terms, that it admits of an ambiguous interpretation; for it may be right, or it may be wrong, according to the different circumſtances of caſes.

Nevertheleſs, the characters of the very eminent and worthy perſons who ſubſcribed this opinion, are ſuch, that it is not poſſible to conceive, that the leaſt equivocation was really intended: ſo that I am entirely at a loſs how to account for their having contented themſelves with ſtating the caſe merely on one ſide of the queſtion (I mean in favour of the maſters,) without ſignifying at the ſame time, that their opinion was only *conditional*, and *not abſolute*. The want of this neceſſary diſtinction, has occaſioned an unjuſt preſumption and prejudice (plainly inconſiſtent with the laws of the realm) againſt the other ſide of the queſtion.

Therefore, with all the deference due to the great learning, ſkill and abilities of theſe very reſpectable perſonages, I propoſe, 1ſt of all, to ſhew, that this opinion *conditionally* is right. And 2dly, That the

general

general preſumption upon the whole is wrong.

The opinion conſiſts of three Parts, 1ſt, "*That a Slave, by coming from the Weſt* "*Indies to Great Britain or Ireland, either* "*with or without his maſter, doth not be*-"*come free, and that his Maſter's property* "*or right in him, is not thereby determined* "*or váried*:" all this is certainly true, provided the Maſter can produce an authentic agreement or "*contract in writing*;" by which it ſhall appear, that the ſaid Slave hath voluntarily bound himſelf, without compulſion or illegal dureſs.

2dly, They affirm, "*That Baptiſm doth* "*not beſtow freedom on him*" (the Slave) "*nor make any alteration in his temporal* "*condition in theſe kingdoms.*" This I am willing for the preſent to allow, as I have not hitherto ſeen any ſufficient authorities to alledge againſt it.

The 3d Part of the opinion is, "*That* "*his*" (the Slave's) "*maſter may legally* "*compel him to return again to the planta*-"*tions.*" This is certainly true, provided that the Maſter is poſſeſſed of ſuch an agreement or contract, as is before mentioned.

For

For even if a free Engliſh Subject ſhould enter into ſuch a kind of contract; he may be carried out of the kingdom (if the contract expreſſes ſo much) *with or without his own ſubſequent conſent* *, by expreſs permiſſion of an Engliſh Statute; (31 Car. II. ch. 2. ſect. xiii.) unleſs the maſter, to ſecure his bargain, ſhall have impriſoned or confined him; for ſuch an act ought, in ſtrict juſtice, to be eſteemed abſolutely illegal, if the indentured Perſon did not previouſly refuſe to fulfil the contract on his part.

Baron Puffendorf, in his Law of Nature and Nations (b. vi. ch. iii. p. 619.) makes ſome obſervations, which may ſerve to illuſtrate this point. "*When a Slave*" (ſays he) "not by way of puniſhment, or on "account of any preceding offence, is "thrown into irons OR OTHERWISE DE-"PRIVED OF CORPORAL LIBERTY, he is "by this act, *releaſed* from his *former ob-"ligations by compact*; for his maſter is "ſup-

* This indeed is law, but whether or not, 'tis altogether equity, doth not reſt with me to determine. The learned Baron Monteſquieu, indeed, ſeems clearly to prove, that a freeman cannot make an equitable bargain for his liberty. "Il n'eſt pas vrai qu'un homme libre puiſſe ſe vendre, &c." b. xv. ch. ii. p. 342.

" ſuppoſed to take off his *moral bonds*, by " thus impoſing *natural.*"

Perhaps the ſtrict regard which the Attorney and Sollicitor General had to the ſecurity of private property, might prevent them from expreſſing in their opinion, how far a Negro Slave in England (not contracted as above) is entitled to the protection of the laws, leſt the knowledge of ſuch a claim of protection ſhould invalidate the maſter's *right of property*, who purchaſed or brought him to England, and who would thereby be liable to be diveſted of the ſaid property.

This certainly ſeems to be a very equitable conſideration; but the ſame equity, as in a caſe between *man* and *man*, obliges us likewiſe to diſtinguiſh how far one man may lawfully be conſidered as the property of another, " *within this kingdom of England, dominion of Wales, or town of Berwick upon Tweed,*" when there is no ſuch previous contract.

The Laws of the Realm do moſt certainly ſecure to every man, without exception, his *private property*; but it muſt be likewiſe remembered, that the nature of every kind of *property* ought to be conſidered,

dered, before it can be lawfully claimed: for there are many cafes wherein *property* is *abfolutely altered*; as in the cafe of contraband goods brought to England, and in all forfeitures, efcheats, and other circumftances, wherein the King's right lawfully interferes.

Salvo Jure Regis, is an exception that takes place of all private claims. Therefore, if a Slave by coming into England, is any ways "*bounden*" in allegiance to the King and the laws, during his refidence within the realm, he becomes *the King's fubject*, which I fhall clearly prove hereafter. The effect of this is, that in *a relative fenfe*, he becomes likewife *the King's property*, according to the law of nations. Baron Puffendorf is very exprefs in this particular, b. vi. ch. iii. p. 614. "*Every Sovereign*" (fays he) "may indeed, as Mr. Hobbes "remarks, fay of *his fubject*, *Hic meus eft*; "*This man is my property*, yet it is in a "quite *different fenfe* that we call a *thing* "our own."

But thofe perfons, who claim their Negro Servants in England, as Slaves, and *private property*, feem in general to have entirely laid afide this proper diftinction. They

They call them, indeed, *Negro Fellows*; but ſo contemptuous is their manner of expreſſion, that the proper meaning of the word *Fellow*, ſeems with them to be entirely reverſed! Their actions correſpond but too well with their addreſs; for they uſurp as an abſolute authority over theſe their *fellow men*, as if they thought them, mere *things*, horſes, dogs, &c.

I have too much reaſon to charge them with this inhumanity; for, in the caſe (wherein I am at preſent concerned) of a Negro being SOLD, during an unlawful confinement, without a warrant, in the Poultry-Compter, though he had been ſet at liberty from the inſupportable tyranny of his maſter (THE SELLER) more than two years before, at a meeting of the Middleſex Juſtices, yet it has been alledged by the ſaid *Seller* (even after the Negro had been a ſecond time ſet at liberty by the authority of the right honourable the Lord Mayor) that he, the ſaid Negro, is *as much private property as a horſe or a dog*.

In anſwer to ſuch unnatural, though uſual compariſons, I might AS REASONABLY ALLEDGE, *(if no regard is to be paid to human nature)* that the Negro ought rather to be ranked

ranked among creatures " *Feræ naturæ*", (pardon, for the preſent, the abſurdity of ſuch an idea) than among horſes, dogs, cats, &c. becauſe thoſe of the latter claſs are eſteemed in law, as " *things of a baſe nature,*" which, it ſeems, the former are not; and therefore (if it can be thought at all allowable to rank a man with beaſts) the Negro has an undoubted right to be eſteemed of the more noble kind of the two. Alſo, for another reaſon, he is entitled to be eſteemed, rather a creature *feræ naturæ*, than of a *baſe nature*; becauſe he was not born in ſlavery (as are many unhappy perſons in the Engliſh plantations) but was *free* born; of human, not baſe, parents; parents, who had as much right to their *natural liberty*, as the wild animals, with which their native country (Africa) abounds: therefore if this Negro ſhould unjuſtly be denied all *human privileges*, yet, as he is not of a *baſe nature*, he ought at leaſt to enjoy as much privilege as bears, hawks, or any other creatures *feræ naturæ*, which have been taken and made tame: becauſe in theſe " *we have only a property*" (ſays Wood, b. ii. ch. 5. p. 539.) " *ſo long as they remain tame, and do not re-*

" *gain*

"*gain their natural liberty, and have not a custom of returning*;" for otherwise they cannot be claimed as an *absolute property* *.

Thus it must appear, that the plea of *private property* in a Negro, as in *a horse or a dog*, is very insufficient and defective. But I will now shew, that the comparing of a man to a beast, at any rate, is unnatural and unjust; as well as the seizing, and detaining him as such, is dangerous to the pretended proprietors. For they cannot be justified, unless they shall be able to prove, that a Negro Slave is neither man, woman nor child †: and if they are not able to do this, how can they presume to consider such a person as a mere "*chose in action*"? or *thing* to be demanded in action?

The Negro must be divested of his humanity, and rendered incapable of the

* "One may have an *absolute property* in hens, geese, ducks, peacocks, &c. but not in creatures that are *Feræ naturæ*, as wild beasts, &c. Id. p. 538.

† Il est impossible que nous supposions que ces gens-la soient des hommes; parceque si nous les supposiions des hommes, on commenceroit à croire que nous NE SOMMES PAS NOUS-MEMES CHRETIENS. L'Esprit des Loix. b. xv. ch. 5. "It is impossible for us to suppose that "these people are *men*; because if we should suppose "them to be *men*, one would begin to believe that *we* "*ourselves are not Christians.*" A very severe (and alas! but too just) satire against Slave-holders!

King's

King's protection, before ſuch an action can lawfully * take place.

But how is he to be diveſted of his *human nature?* or of his juſt right to the King's protection?

A man may, indeed, be ſaid to be diveſted of his *humanity*, 1ſt, in a moral ſenſe, by his own action, in ſtooping to any kind of baſeneſs beneath the dignity of a *man*. And 2dly, By the execution of the laws, in puniſhment of ſome particular kinds of baſeneſs, for which a man may *lawfully* be diveſted of his humanity by a *civil death:* that is; may be "*diſabled to* "*hold any office or franchiſe*, &c." "*as* "*if ſuch perſon was naturally dead.*" This is one of the penalties expreſſed in a Statute (2 Geo. II. ch. 24.) againſt bribery and corruption in Parliamentary Elections, whereby, not leſs the *Briber* than the *Bribed*, (whether the offence be committed "*by himſelf, or any perſon employed by him*") is ſubjected to the diveſture abovementioned. But the vileſt and moſt ignorant Negro Slaves are not ſo *inhumanly* baſe and

* Trover lies not for a Negro: for men may be owners, and therefore not the ſubject of property, &c. See Cunningham's Law Dictionary, under the wcrd Negro.

degenerate

degenerate as these Time-servers, who offend against God! the King! their friends and fellow-subjects! themselves! and all their unhappy posterity, even the children that are unborn! They are enemies to the State, infinitely more to be dreaded, than the most puissant foreign power at open war! *

* No shuffling arts or equivocations whatsoever can lighten this monstrous load of guilt, for which the offenders must *one day* most certainly be called to account, notwithstanding that they may have escaped the penalties of this English Statute: for indeed it is merely the penalties (or execution) of the said Statute which they escape and not the guilt of breaking it; because the same is so warily drawn up, that there is not the least room for mental reservation.

A very large proportion of the freeholders in this kingdom, it is to be feared, are involved in this horrid guilt! Nay every elector who hath but even EAT or DRANK at the expence of another, during the time of an election, is likewise in some measure guilty! (though charity will incline us to suppose that their offence is, for the most part, occasioned by ignorance, rather than wilful corruption) for not only money, but also any "Gift, Office, Employment, or OTHER REWARD "WHATSOEVER" is forbid by the said Act. Now this prohibition must necessarily include *meat* and *drink*, since these articles cannot be considered below the estimation of a "REWARD," because they are expresly prohibited by a preceding Act still in force, (viz. 7 W. III. ch. 4.) whereby those Candidates, who shall "*directly* or *indirectly* give, present or allow to any per-"son or persons, having voice or vote in such election, "any money, MEAT, DRINK, ENTERTAINMENT, or "PROVISION, &c. are rendered incapable (though "elected) *to act*, *sit*, *or have any vote*, *or place in parlia-"ment*, &c." Happy would it be for England, if this

But the caſe of this poor Negro is very different. If he is a Slave, yet it was not with his own conſent that he was made ſo. He neither *ſold himſelf*, nor has he *betrayed others*, and cannot therefore be liable to ſuch ſevere penalties. He has not been guilty of any offences, that I know of, for which he might *lawfully be diveſted of his humanity*; and therefore it muſt certainly be allowed, that he differs from a horſe or a dog in this very *eſſential point*, viz. *his humanity*.

ſalutary law could be ſtrictly enforced! Bribes in money, places, &c. are not productive of half ſo much evil, as the debaucheries of election entertainments, becauſe the pernicious effects of the latter are ſo permanent, that they may fairly be ſaid to be tranſmitted from election to election. The groſs immorality, as well as the deplorable idleneſs and poverty, (all forerunners of ſlavery) which too much prevail in many parts of this kingdom, ought, (I ſincerely believe) to be principally attributed to the unlawful practice of opening houſes for public entertainment at elections: and we cannot hope that this dangerous evil will ever be corrected, unleſs the wiſdom of the legiſlature ſhall hereafter think fit to oblige every candidate (as ſoon as he declares himſelf ſuch) to promiſe upon oath, that he will ſtrictly obſerve every article of the laſt mentioned Act, againſt treating electors. This long digreſſion from the ſubject of Negro Slaves, the author hopes may be pardoned, eſpecially, if the reader will pleaſe to conſider, that civil and political Slavery, as well as Slavery to ſenſual appetites, are ſo very nearly connected with each other, in their nature and effects, that it is no very conſiderable tranſition from the preſent point, to ſpeak of them together.

So

So that, though he may have been a Slave, and, (according to the cuſtom of the Colonies) accounted the *private property* of his maſter, before he came to England, yet theſe circumſtances make no alteration in *his human nature*; for every Negro Slave, being undoubtedly either man, woman, or child; he or ſhe, immediately upon their arrival in England, becomes *the King's property* in the *relative ſenſe* before-mentioned, and *cannot*, therefore, be "*out of* "*the King's protection*."

But if any Slaveholder ſtill obſtinately perſiſts in his claim of *private property*, let him be no longer ignorant, that "*where* "*the title of the King and a common Perſon* "*concurs, the title of the King ſhall be* "*preferred.*" Wood's Inſtit. b. i. ch. 2. p. 32.

Let him know, likewiſe, that the quondam Slave is enabled by the laws of this realm, to vindicate and put in Suit this title and claim of the King; "for" (ſays Wood, b. iv. ch. iv. p. 938.) "*when any* "*thing is prohibited by a Statute*," (as in this caſe) "though the Statute doth give an "Action or penalty, yet the party grieved "may have an Action, *Tam pro Domino Rege*, "*quam ſeipſo*;" as well for the King, as in his

his own behalf, *for the ſecurity of his perſon*; which is a much more reaſonable and effectual plea, than that of *any private property* whatſoever: for it is an eſtabliſhed maxim of the moſt learned lawyers, eſpecially the great Sir Edward Coke, (1 Inſt. 124b. 2 Inſt. 42. 115.) that "*the law favours liberty, and the freedom of a man from impriſonment; and therefore kind interpretations ſhall be made on its behalf.*" Wood's Inſt. b. i. ch. i. p. 25.

But ſome perſons have alledged, that a Slave cannot avail himſelf of the laws, becauſe he is not *a ſubject*; for a Slave (ſay they) cannot, in a political ſenſe, be conſidered as a ſubject; but I hope ſoon to make it appear otherwiſe. I have already ſhewn, that an Engliſh *ſubject* may be made a Slave by contract; but it is neceſſary to obſerve likewiſe, that no contract whatſoever, *can untie his indiſpenſable obligation and allegiance to the King and the laws.* Therefore as it appears, that a *ſubject* may become *a Slave*; ſo it neceſſarily follows, that *a Slave* may be *a ſubject*, ſince the Ties of allegiance cannot be diſſolved.

An Engliſh *ſubject* cannot be made *a Slave*, without *his own free conſent*, as I have

have before obſerved, but, on the other hand, a foreign *Slave* is made *a ſubject*, with or without his own conſent: there needs no contract for this purpoſe, as in the other caſe, nor any other act or deed whatſoever, but that of his being landed in England; " For *every Alien and Stranger* " *born out of the King's obeiſance, not being* " *denizen, which now or hereafter*" (ſays a Statute of 32 Hen. viii. ch. xvi. ſect. ix.) " *ſhall come in or to this realm, or elſewhere* " *within the King's dominions, ſhall, after* " *the ſaid firſt of September, next coming, be* " *bounden by and unto the Laws and Statutes* " *of this realm,* and to all and ſingular the " contents of the ſame."

Now it muſt be obſerved, that this law makes no diſtinction of *bond or free*; neither of colours or complexions, whether of *black, brown,* or *white*; for " *every alien and ſtranger*" (without exception) " *are* " *bounden by and unto the laws, &c.*"

This *binding* or *obligation*, is properly expreſſed by the Engliſh word *Ligeance* (a Ligando) which may be " *either perpetual* " *or temporary*:" (Wood, b. i. c. iii. p. 37.) but one or other of theſe is indiſpenſably due to the Sovereign from all ranks

 and

and conditions of people. Their being "*bounden nnto the laws,*" (upon which the Sovereign's right is founded) expreſſes and implies their SUBJECTION to the laws; and therefore to alledge, that an Alien is not a SUBJECT, becauſe he is in bondage, is not only a plea without foundation, but a contradiction in terms; for every perſon, who in any reſpect is in *ſubjection* to the laws, muſt undoubtedly be a *ſubject*.

Foreign Ambaſſadors, indeed, by the Law of Nations, enjoy peculiar privileges; which are alſo confirmed by a Statute of 7 Ann, ch. 12. as well as the privileges of their ſervants; though the latter cannot claim them, unleſs their names are regiſtered in the Secretaries Office, &c. purſuant to the ſaid Statute.

Neverthelеſs, even an Ambaſſador is, in ſome degree, *ſubject* to the laws of this realm; for if ſuch a one "*is guilty of* "*treaſon againſt the King's life, he may be* "*condemned and executed,* but for *other* "*treaſons,* he ſhall be ſent home, with a "demand to puniſh him, or to ſend him "back to be puniſhed." Wood's Inſt. b. iii. ch. i. p. 588. Ambaſſadors could not be ſaid to be guilty of *treaſon*, if they were not

not conſidered as "*bounden*" by a ſort of *temporary allegiance* to the King, in return for his protection, and that of the public faith, during their reſidence in this kingdom.

I come now to the main point in queſtion; for as I have proved, not only that there are different degrees of *ſubjection* in England, but alſo, that *bondmen* may be *ſubjects* as well as *freemen*, the inevitable concluſion upon the whole is, that *every man, woman, or child,* "*that now is, or* "*hereafter ſhall be an inhabitant or reſiant* "*of this kingdom of England, dominion of* "*Wales, or town of Berwick upon Tweed,*" is in ſome reſpect or other the *King's ſubject*; and, *as ſuch*, is abſolutely ſecure in his or her *perſonal liberty*, by virtue of a Statute, 31 Car. II. ch. ii. and particularly, by the xiith Section of the ſame, (a copy of which is hereunto annexed) wherein *ſubjects of all conditions* are plainly included.

This Act is expreſly intended "for the "better ſecuring *the liberty of* THE SUB-"JECT, and for prevention of impriſon-"ment beyond the ſeas." It contains no diſtinctions of *natural-born, naturalized, de-*

 nizen,

nizen, or *alien ſubjects*, nor of *white* or *black, free men, or even of* BOND-MEN (except in the caſe already mentioned of *a contract in writing, allowed by the* 13th Section, and the exception likewiſe in the 14th Section, concerning felons) but they are all included under the general titles of " *the ſubject*," " ANY OF *the ſaid ſubjects*," " *every ſuch* " *perſon, &c.*" Now the definition of the word " PERSON, *in its relative or civil ca-* ' *pacity*," (according to Wood, b. i. c. ii. " p. 27.) *is either the King or a ſubject*." Theſe are the *only capital diſtinctions* that can be made; though the latter conſiſts of a variety of denominations and degrees: therefore perhaps it may be a dangerous point to advance, that any perſon whatſoever in England, beſides the King, is not *a ſubject*; leſt the ſame ſhould be conſtrued as a breach of the Statute 23 Eliz. ch. i. (*intitled an Act to retain the Queen's Majeſty's ſubjects in their due obedience*) whereby " *all* " *perſons whatſoever*" are liable to the penalties of the ſaid Act, who " have, *or* " *ſhall have, or ſhall pretend to have power*, " or ſhall by any ways or means put " in practice to abſolve, perſuade, or *with-* " *draw any* of the Queen's Majeſty's ſub-

" jects,

" jects, or *any* within her Highness's " realms and dominions *from their natural* " *obedience to her Majesty*." &c. sect. ii.

But if I were even to allow that a *Negro Slave* is not a subject (though I think I have clearly proved that he is) yet it is plain, that such an one ought not to be denied the benefit of the King's courts, unless the Slaveholder shall be able to prove, likewise, that he is not A MAN; because " EVERY " MAN may be *free* to sue for and *defend* " *his right* in our *courts*" (says a Statute 20 Edw. III. ch. iv.) " and elsewhere according to law." " And NO MAN of *what* " *estate* or *condition* that he be" (here can be no exception whatsoever) " shall be " put out of land or tenement, NOR TA-" KEN, NOR IMPRISONED, nor disinhe-" rited, nor put to death, without being " brought in answer *by due process of the* " *law*." 28 Edw. III. ch. iii.

" No MAN," therefore, " *of what estate* " *or condition that he be*," can lawfully be detained in England as a slave, because we have *no law* whereby a man *may be condemned to slavery*, without his own consent, (for even convicted felons must " *in open court*

" *pray*

"*pray to be tranſported* *) and therefore there cannot be any "*due proceſs* † *of the law,*" tending to ſo baſe a purpoſe: it follows therefore, that every man who preſumes to detain any perſon whatſoever as a Slave, otherwiſe than by virtue of a written contract, acts manifeſtly without "*due proceſs of the* "*law,*" and conſequently is liable to the Slave's "*action of falſe impriſonment,*" becauſe "EVERY MAN *may be free to ſue*, &c." ſo that the Slaveholder cannot avail himſelf of his imaginary *property*, either by the aſſiſtance of the Common Law, or of a Court of Equity; for in both, his ſuit will certainly appear unjuſt and indefenſible. The former cannot aſſiſt him, becauſe the ſtatute law at preſent is ſo far from ſuppoſing any man in a ſtate of Slavery, that it cannot even permit ſuch a ſtate, except in the two caſes mentioned in the 13th and 14th Section of the Habeas Corpus Act; and the Courts of Equity, likewiſe, muſt neceſſarily decide againſt him, becauſe his

* See Habeas Corpus Act, Sect. 14.

† An eminent Lawyer who read this book in MS. wrote the following ſenſible remark therein, viz. "If force cannot be uſed, without *legal proceſs*, what "*proceſs* can a maſter obtain to uſe that force? and "therefore how legally compel any man to depart the "kingdom?"

mere

mere mercenary plea of *private property*, cannot *equitably* (in a caſe between *man and man)* ſtand in competition with that *ſuperior property*, which every man muſt neceſſarily be allowed to have in his own *proper perſon*.

How then is the Slaveholder to ſecure what he eſteems his *property?* Perhaps he will endeavour clandeſtinely to ſeize the ſuppoſed Slave in order to tranſport him (" *with or without his conſent*") to the colonies where ſuch *property* is allowed. But let him take care what he does; the *very attempt* is puniſhable *; and even the making over his *property* to another for *that purpoſe*, renders him equally liable to the ſevere penalties of the law; for a bill of ſale may certainly be included under the terms expreſſed in the Habeas Corpus Act, (12th Sect.) viz. " *any warrant or writing*

* Nevertheleſs, I have heard ſome perſons adviſe the employing of ruffians or thief-takers for this purpoſe, with as much confidence, as if they were adviſing a regular proceeding at law, not ſeeming to have the leaſt idea of the horrid diſhoneſty, and dangerous tendency of ſuch violent meaſures: for no man can be ſafe, if ſuch *unlawful* practices eſcape with impunity; becauſe they, who kidnap Negroes, are not leſs guilty in the eye of the law, than thoſe who kidnap white men; and frequent practices againſt the liberty of the former, will certainly facilitate attempts againſt the latter.

" *for*

" *for ſuch commitment, detainer, impriſon-* " *ment, or tranſportation,* &c."

It is alſo dangerous for a counſellor or any other perſon, *to adviſe* (ſee the Act " *ſhall be adviſing,*") ſuch a proceeding by ſaying, " that *a maſter may legally compel* " *him (the Slave) to return again to the* " *Plantations.*" Likewiſe an Attorney, Notary Publick, or any other perſon, who ſhall preſume to draw up, negotiate, or *even to witneſs* a bill of ſale, or other inſtrument for ſuch commitment, &c. offends equally againſt this law; becauſe, " All or " any perſon or perſons, that ſhall *frame,* " *contrive, write, ſeal, or counterſign* ANY " WARRANT OR WRITING for ſuch com- " mitment, *detainer, impriſonment, or tranſ-* " *portation,* or ſhall be ADVISING, aiding, or " aſſiſting in the ſame, *or any of them*;" are liable to all the penalties of the act, " *And* " *the plaintif in every ſuch action, ſhall have* " *judgment to recover* his *treble coſts,* beſides " *damages*; which damages, ſo to be given, " ſhall not be leſs than *five hundred pounds*;" ſo that the injured may have ample ſatisfaction for their ſufferings. And even a Judge may not direct or inſtruct the jury, contrary to this Statute, whatſoever his *private* *opinion*

opinion may be concerning *property* in Slaves; becauſe, "*no order or command,* "*nor no injunction*" is allowed to interfere with this golden Act of liberty.

Some have thought that the word *injunction* does not relate to the dictating of a Judge, but to the mandate of the Lord Chancellor, which is ſometimes iſſued to prevent the recovery of exceſſive damages. But this does not remove the force of the above-mentioned obſervation; for if the interpoſition of *equity* is not permitted, ſo that the *injunction*, even of a Lord Chancellor, cannot remove the literal force of this law, 'tis certain that the injunction of an inferior judge (who is more particularly bound by *the letter of the law*) ought not to avail any thing.

Now if all theſe things be conſidered, I think, we may ſafely prefer the ſentiment of that excellent lawyer Lord Chief Juſtice Holt, (before quoted) to all contrary opinions, viz. that "*as ſoon as a Negro* "*comes into England, he becomes free.*" Salkeld's Reports, Vol. ii. p. 666.

END OF THE FIRST PART.

PART

Extract from a Statute intituled, " An " Act for the better securing the " Liberty of *the subject*, and for " Prevention of Imprisonment be- " yond the Seas." Anno trice- simo primo Caroli secundi Regis. A. D. 1679.

Ch. II. Sect. XII.

AND for preventing illegal imprisonments in prisons beyond the seas; (2) be it further enacted by the authority aforesaid, that *no subject* of this realm that now is, or hereafter shall be an inhabitant or resiant of this kingdom of England, dominion of Wales, or town of Berwick upon Tweed, shall or may be *sent prisoner* into Scotland, Ireland,

Ireland, Jerfey, Guernfey, Tangier, or into parts, garrifons, *iflands, or places beyond the feas*, which are, or at any time hereafter fhall be within or without the dominions of his Majefty, his heirs or fucceffors; (3) and that *every fuch imprifonment* is hereby enacted and adjudged to be illegal; (4) andthat if *any of the faid fubjects now is*, or hereafter fhall be fo imprifoned, *every fuch perfon* and perfon fo imprifoned, fhall and may for every fuch imprifonment, *maintain by virtue of this act, an action or actions* of falfe imprifonment, in any of his Majefty's courts of record, againft the perfon or perfons by whom he or fhe fhall be fo *committed, detained, imprifoned, fent prifoner or tranfported*, contrary to the true meaning of this Act, and againft *all or any perfon or perfons* that fhall *frame, contrive, write, feal or counterfign* any warrant *or writing* for fuch *commitment, detainer, imprifonment, or tranfportation*, or fhall be *advifing, aiding or affifting* in the fame, or *any of them*; (5) and the plaintiff in every fuch action fhall have judgment to *recover his treble cofts*, befides *damages*; which damages fo to be given, fhall not be lefs than five hundred pounds; (6) in which action, no delay, ftay, or ftop

 of

of proceeding by rule, order or command, nor no injunction, protection or privilege whatsoever, nor any more than one imparlance shall be allowed, excepting such rule of the court wherein the action shall depend, made in open court, as shall be thought in justice necessary, for special cause to be expressed in the said rule; (7) and the person or persons who shall *knowingly frame, contrive, write, seal or countersign any warrant* for such *commitment, detainer* or transportation, or shall so *commit, detain, imprison* or *transport any* person or persons contrary to this act, or be *any ways advising, aiding or assisting* therein, being lawfully convicted thereof, shall be disabled from thenceforth to bear any office of trust or profit within the said realm of England, dominion of Wales, or town of Berwick upon Tweed, or any of the islands, territories or dominions thereunto belonging; (8) and shall incur and sustain the pains, penalties and forfeitures limited, ordained and provided in and by the statute of provision and præmunire, made in the sixteenth year of King Richard the second; (9) and be incapable of any pardon from the King, his heirs or successors, of the

said

ſaid forfeitures, loſſes or diſabilities, or any of them.

XIII. Provided always, that nothing in this act extend to give benefit to any perſon, who ſhall by contract in writing agree with any merchant or owner of any plantation, or other perſon whatſoever, to be tranſported to any parts beyond the ſeas, and receive earneſt upon ſuch agreement, although that afterwards ſuch perſon ſhall renounce ſuch contract.

XIV. Provided always, and be it enacted, that if any perſon or perſons lawfully convicted of any felony, ſhall, in open court, pray to be tranſported beyond the ſeas, and the court ſhall think fit to leave him or them in priſon for that purpoſe, ſuch perſon or perſons may be tranſported into any parts beyond the ſeas; this Act, or any thing therein contained to the contrary notwithſtanding.

XVII. (Memorandum) Proſecution to be made within two years.

PART II.

The Anſwer to an Objection which has been made to the foregoing Remarks.

AN objection has been made to the foregoing remarks, viz. "That Negro Slaves "are moſt certainly a ſet of people whom "the Legiſlature had not in conſideration or "contemplation, at the time of making the "ſeveral ſtatutes quoted in their favour;" and indeed this obſervation ſeems not to be without ſome foundation, for Lord Chief Juſtice Powell declared, that "*the law* "*takes no notice of a Negro.*" (Holt's Reports, fol. 495.) We are therefore now to conſider, firſt, Whether or not it be eſteemed a defect in our laws, that general and comprehenſive

prehenſive terms are uſed inſtead of a particular recital of every rank and denomination of people who form the community? And ſecondly, whether any rank or denomination of people can be rendered either exempt from the penalties of the laws, or excluded from their protection on account of their not being particularly mentioned therein?

I have before obſerved, that the general term "EVERY ALIEN," includes *all ſtrangers whatſoever*, and renders them *ſubject* to the King and the laws during their reſidence in this kingdom; and this is certainly true, whether the aliens be Turks, Moors, Arabians, Tartars, or even Savages from any part of the world.

On the other hand, if we were to ſuppoſe, that a particular recital of each denomination of ſtrangers is neceſſary, we ſhould render the laws extremely vague and uncertain; for ſuch a recital would not only be intolerably tedious, but ſubject to many omiſſions, and ſuch a continual want of additions as would render them ineffectual in many unforeſeen caſes; whereas the ſhort general term before-mentioned, muſt forever remain comprehenſive and effectual;

becaufe penal laws for fecuring the peace, and enforcing morality, are ufually calculated to laft forever, and are, therefore, neceffarily expreffed in fuch general terms, that (as far as human prudence can devife) they may guard againft all poffible cafes of the particular vices which they refpectively prohibit.

Indeed the nature of the offence prohibited, (as well as the penalty) ought to be very particularly expreffed, but it is always time enough to particularize an offender, when there is fufficient proof againft any one.

Men are rendered obnoxious to the laws, by their offences, and not by the particular denomination of their rank, order, parentage, colour or country; and therefore, though we fhould fuppofe, that any particular body of people whatfoever were not known, or had in confideration by the Legiflature at the different times when the feveral penal laws were made, yet no one can reafonably conceive, that fuch men are exempted on this account from the penalties of the faid laws, when legally convicted of having offended againft them.

Laws calculated for the moral purpoſe of preventing oppreſſion, are likewiſe uſually ſuppoſed to be everlaſting, and to make up a part of our happy conſtitution: for which reaſon, though the kind of oppreſſion to be guarded againſt, and the penalties for offenders are minutely deſcribed therein, yet the perſons to be protected are comprehended in terms as general as poſſible, that "no perſon *who now is*, or "*hereafter ſhall be* an inhabitant or re-"ſiant in this kingdom," (ſee Habeas Corpus Act, ſect. xii.) may ſeem to be excluded from protection.

The general terms of the ſeveral ſtatutes before-cited are ſo full and clear, that they admit of no exception whatſoever, for all perſons (Negroes as well as others) muſt be included in the terms—"the SUBJECT; "—NO SUBJECT OF THIS REALM THAT "NOW IS OR HEREAFTER SHALL BE AN "INHABITANT, &c.—ANY SUBJECT; "—*every ſuch perſon*. See Habeas Corpus "Act. Alſo EVERY MAN may be FREE "to ſue, &c. 20 Edward III. cap. iv. and "NO MAN, of WHAT ESTATE OR CON-"DITION THAT HE BE, ſhall be—*taken* "*nor impriſoned*, &c."

If this be duly conſidered, I hope it will be granted, that all ſuch general expreſſions ought to be allowed their due weight, according to the literal meaning of the words, (eſpecially in all caſes wherein the relief of a man from oppreſſion is the object) otherwiſe the ſenſe of the legiſlature would be continually liable to the perverſions of intereſted or capricious perſons.

Would it not be eſteemed a great injuſtice, if any one was to alledge, that a Hungarian, Pole, Muſcovite, or alien of any other European nation, is not protected by our laws when in England, becauſe there is a poſſibility of ſuppoſing, that his countrymen might not have been "*had in* "*conſideration or contemplation* at the time "of making theſe laws?"

Now, if this be granted with reſpect to the more civilized nations, why not to all others?

True juſtice makes no reſpect of perſons, and can never deny to any one that bleſſing to which all mankind have an undoubted right, their *natural liberty*.

Though the law makes no mention of Negro Slaves, yet this is no juſt argument for excluding them from the general protection of our happy conſtitution.

Neither can the objection, that Negro Slaves were not " *had in conſideration or " contemplation" when theſe laws were made*, prove any thing againſt them; but on the contrary much in their favour; for both theſe circumſtances are ſtrong preſumptive proofs, that *the practice* of importing Slaves into this kingdom, and retaining them as ſuch, is an innovation entirely foreign to the ſpirit and intention of the laws now in force.

This will plainly appear when we conſider, that if the importing and retaining of Negroes or others in a ſtate of Slavery, had formerly been permitted in this kingdom, and if the legiſlature had really intended to countenance the ſame, a particular exception to that purpoſe would certainly have been inſerted; becauſe it is (and ever was) well known, that when there are no particular exceptions, the general terms of ſtatutes muſt have their due weight.

Now if Slavery in this kingdom is really an innovation unknown in law, (I mean in the laws * now in force) how can the vul-

* The intolerable and unjuſt laws relating to vaſſalage and villenage, have long been obſolete, and cannot afford

gar plea *of private property in a Slave, as in a horſe or a dog*, avail any thing either in equity or law?

It cannot avail in equity, becauſe the liberty of the meaneſt individual is of much more value and conſideration to himſelf, than any other kind of private property whatſoever can be to another, and therefore his plea in behalf of his own natural liberty is much more reaſonable, and ought certainly to be preferred (as I have already obſerved) before the Slavemonger's mere mercenary claim of private property in his perſon.

Neither at common law can the latter be recoverable, for Slavery being an innovation entirely foreign to the ſpirit and intention of the preſent laws, as is before remarked, there is *no law* to juſtify proceedings, nor ſufficient precedents to authorize judgment.

Nay, it is an innovation of ſuch an unwarrantable and dangerous nature, that beſides the groſs infringement of the common and natural rights of mankind, it is plainly *coutrary* to the laws and conſtitu-

afford the leaſt plea for the Slaveholder's juſtification. See part iv.

tion

tion of this kingdom; for I have ſhewn, (even from the objection of thoſe who differ from me in opinion) that no laws whatſover countenance it, and (by my own quotations from the ſtatutes) that ſeveral in the cleareſt though *general* terms render it actionable.

The moſt dangerous conſequences may be expected, if the expreſs letter and force of the law is permitted in any caſe whatſoever, to be annulled by the *private opinions* of council; but more particularly when *civil liberty* is concerned. I do not mean however to cenſure *opinions* in general, but only ſuch as are oppoſed to the laws of the land; and I hope it will be allowed with reſpect to *my own opinion* in particular, that it is not founded on my own preſumption, but on the plaineſt *literal expreſſions* of ſtatutes, formed and ordained by the wiſdom and authority of King, Lords, and Commons.

October 9, 1767.

GRANVILLE SHARP.

END OF THE SECOND PART.

PART

PART III.

An examination of the Advantages and Disadvantages of tolerating SLAVERY *in England.*

IN the two former parts of this work, I have attempted to demonſtrate, that Slavery is an innovation in England, contrary to the ſpirit and intention of our preſent laws and conſtitution. If this opinion be admitted, the following points do, of courſe, demand the ſerious conſideration of the public.

1ſt. How far this *innovation* may be eſteemed neceſſary? or whether there are any ſingular advantages attending it, which ſhould engage us to favour the eſtabliſh-

ment

ment of it here, in direct oppoſition both to *law and equity?* And 2dly, Whether the ſame is not liable, on the other hand, to be attended with ſome ſuch unavoidable miſchiefs, as would much over-balance any advantages that can poſſibly be propoſed or expected from it?

The only reaſonable plea that is uſually alledged, for the neceſſity of Slavery in England, is the ſecurity of private property; for it would be unjuſt (ſay the advocates for Slavery) that the maſter's property or right in Slaves, ſhould be determined or varied, by their coming from the Weſt Indies to England.

But before this plea be admitted, we ought to conſider the maſter's reaſon for bringing a Slave to England.

It cannot be for the ſake of a market, to make his money of him, becauſe a ſtout young Negro, who can read and write, and is approved of in domeſtic ſervice, is ſold for no more than thirty pounds * in

* The Negro, whoſe liberty the author procured by the authority of the Lord Mayor, was ſold in the Poultry Compter for *thirty pounds*; being firſt unlawfully confined there by the *Seller*, without any warrant whatſoever, and afterwards as unlawfully retained for ſeveral days by order of *the Buyer*; both *Buyer* and *Seller* therefore,

England; whereas it is certain, that ſuch a one might be ſold, at leaſt, for the ſame ſum in the Weſt Indies; and ſometimes, perhaps, for near double the money, ſo that a Slave from thence, not only loads his owner with an additional charge for freight, but is brought to a much worſe market.

It is plain therefore, that trade cannot be materially affected, by the putting a ſtop to ſuch clandeſtine and unnatural traffic.

And further, if the maſter brings his Slaves to England, for the ſake of their domeſtic ſervices only, and not for ſale, he cannot be ſaid to be really injured, when they regain their liberty; becauſe I will make it appear hereafter, that he may be ſerved, during his ſtay in England, full as well, and with as little expence, by free Engliſh ſervants, as he could poſſibly be by his own Slaves, even if the law would permit him to keep them as ſuch.

therefore, as well as *all their accomplices*, are certainly liable to very ſevere penalties for falſe impriſonment; but the author is rather deſirous to inſtruct theſe offenders, than to adviſe a proſecution againſt them, becauſe the parties themſelves (he thinks) are not ſo much to blame, as thoſe Lawyers whoſe miſtaken opinions are the original cauſes of ſuch ſhameful outrages.

But

But ſuppoſe the maſter, by the prejudices of a Weſt Indian education, is ſo capricious and depraved, that he prefers the conſtrained ſervice of Slaves to the willing attendance of freemen. Or rather, let us ſuppoſe another caſe, viz.

That a Weſt Indian gentleman comes to England on account of his health, and is *obliged* to bring ſome Slaves with him, to attend him during the voyage, and that it might perhaps be very inconvenient to loſe them on his arrival here.

Now in both theſe caſes there is ſtill a remedy left, which may enable the former ſuppoſed perſon to indulge, in ſome meaſure, his capricious humour, and the latter to ſuit his convenience or neceſſity, without infringing further upon the civil liberties of this kingdom, than what the laws will warrant.

For when any Weſt Indian gentleman intends to remove to England, he may undoubtedly find a ſufficient number of his Slaves, that would gladly enter into a *written agreement*, to return to the Weſt Indies from England, when required, merely for the ſake of coming to England.

It

It muſt be remembered however, that a previous manumiſſion will be neceſſary, otherwiſe there can be no legal agreement whatſoever for ſervice; becauſe a Slave who has ſigned an agreement, may afterwards plead *illegal dureſs per minas*, &c. which will effectually invalidate his contract in England. (See the 4th. Part.)

But perhaps it may be objected, that the granting of a manumiſſion is prohibited in the colonies by law. And indeed, the laws of Virginia expreſly ordain, " That no " Negro, Mulatto or Indian Slaves, ſhall " be ſet free, upon any pretence whatſo- " ever, *except* for ſome *meritorious ſervices*, " to be adjudged and allowed by the Go- " vernor and Council, for the time being, " and a licence thereupon firſt had and ob- " tained. And, that where any Slave " ſhall be ſet free by his maſter or owner, " otherwiſe than is herein before directed, " it ſhall and may be lawful for the " church-wardens of the pariſh, wherein " ſuch Negro, Mulatto, or Indian, ſhall " reſide for the ſpace of one month, next " after his or her being ſet free, and they " are hereby authorized and required to " *take up* and SELL the ſaid Negro, Mul-

" latto,

"latto, or Indian, AS SLAVES *, at the "next court held for the ſaid county, by *pub*-"*lic outcry*, &c." † Nevertheleſs I apprehend, that when the ſervice of an approved Slave is become ſo neceſſary to his maſter, that it cannot, without great inconvenience, be diſpenſed with; the ſame ought to be eſteemed a *meritorious ſervice*, ſuch as the Governor and Council cannot reaſonably diſallow.

So that I do not think, a maſter would find any great difficulty in procuring leave to ſet free ſuch perſons, as he ſhould think neceſſary *to carry with him out of the colony*; becauſe no man could object, that the

* The cruelty and injuſtice of this law is too obvious to need any comment. The plea of *ſelf-preſervation* and *public ſecurity* cannot in the leaſt excuſe it, becauſe the ſame cannot juſtify any further proceeding, even in the caſe of an avowed enemy, taken in open war, than the holding the priſoner in ſafe cuſtody, until there can be a convenient opportunity of ranſoming, exchanging or of ſending them away with ſafety to the public, on the concluſion of a peace. But, "to take up and SELL "—AS SLAVES," free perſons, to whoſe ſervices they are not in the leaſt entitled, not having even the vulgar and inſufficient plea of *private property* to alledge; this, I ſay, diſcovers ſuch a ſhameful depravity of mind in the law-makers of that province, as is ſcarcely to be equalled even in Barbary itſelf.

† 9 George I. cap. iv. ſect. xvii. p. 342. of "A "Collection of all the Acts of Aſſembly now in force "in the Colony of Virginia." Printed at Williamſburg 1733.

granting

granting of a manumiſſion in this caſe, is liable to affect the ſafety of the colony, even in the leaſt degree.

But there is ſtill another very obvious and natural objection to be removed, before my propoſal of a contract can poſſibly be admitted, viz. That no Slave, after being once made free, would *willingly* enter again into bondage by ſigning a contract.

This objection would certainly hold good in England, or in any other free country; but the tyrannical conſtitution of the Britiſh colonies (to the indelible diſgrace of the Britiſh name) reduces the freedom of any poor man to ſo low a value, that a bargain for the ſervitude of ſuch a one, by indenture, might be made on very eaſy terms*, ſo far is it from being unnatural, or even uncommon; therefore the ſame objection cannot be ſaid to ſubſiſt in the colonies;

* "Dans tout Gouvernement Deſpotique on a une facilité à ſe vendre; l'Eſclavage Politique y aneantit en quelque façon la Liberté Civile.

Mr. Perry a (*dans l'Etat preſent de la Grande Ruſſie*, Paris, 1717, *in* 12°.) dit que les Moſcovites ſe vendent très aiſément; j'en ſçai bien la raiſon, c'eſt que leur Liberté ne vaut rien.

A Achim tout le monde cherche à ſe vendre. Quelques-uns des principaux (*for which is quoted* "*Nouveau voyage autour du monde par Guill. Dampierre. Tom.* 3, *Amſterdam*, 1711) Seigneurs n'ont pas moins de mille Eſclaves,

for if we consider the cruel and severe restrictions * of the plantation laws, whereby *free*

Esclaves, qui sont des principaux Marchands, qui ont aussi beaucoup d'Esclaves sous eux, et ceux-ci beaucoup d'autres; on en herite et on les fait trafiquer. Dans ces Etats les hommes libres, trop foibles contre le Gouvernement, cherchent à devenir les Esclaves de ceux qui tyrannisent le Gouvernement." De L'Esprit des Loix. L. 15. c. vi. p. 347. Geneve, 8vo.

* —"And also, if any Negro, Mulatto, or *Indian*, "BOND or FREE, shall, at any time, lift his, or her "hand, in opposition against any Christian, not being "Negro, Mulatto, or Indian, he or she so offending, "shall, for every such offence, proved by the oath of "the party, receive on his or her bare back, thirty "lashes, *well laid on*; cognizable by a justice of the "peace of that county wherein such offence shall be "committed." 4 Ann. c. xlix. sect. xxxiv. Acts of Virginia, p. 226.

No allowance is here made for any unjust provocation, which a poor *free* Negro may happen to receive from a licentious, quarrelsome, drunken, or fraudulent white man, who may be pleased to disgrace Christianity, by calling himself *a Christian!*—But peremptorily, if he shall, "at any time (only) *lift his hand in opposition* "against *any Christian*, not being Negro, &c." (howsoever he may have been injured by him)—he—shall "receive on his bare back, thirty lashes, *well laid on*," &c. An intolerable subjection this, for those who are called free! nay it is too base and oppressive to be submitted to even by—Slaves!

Another law (9 Geo. I. c. iv. sect. xiv.) ordains "That no Negro, Mulatto, or Indian whatsoever, "(except as is hereafter excepted) shall hereafter pre-"sume to keep, or carry any gun, powder, shot, or "any club, or other weapon whatsoever, offensive or "(even) DEFENSIVE; but that every gun, and all "powder and shot, and every *such club or weapon*, as "aforesaid, found or taken in the hands, custody, or "possession of any such Negro, Mulatto or *Indian*, shall "be taken away; and upon due proof thereof, made

" before any justice of the peace of the county where " such offence shall be committed, be forfeited to the " seisor and informer; and moreover, every such Ne- " gro, Mulatto or *Indian*, in whose hands, custody " or possession the same shall be found, shall, by order " of the said justice, have and receive any number of " *lashes*, not exceeding thirty-nine, *well laid on*, on his " or her bare back, for every such offence."

Sect. xv. " Provided nevertheless, That every free " Negro, Mulatto or *Indian*, being a *housekeeper*, or " listed in the militia, may be permitted to keep one " gun, powder and shot; and that those who are not " housekeepers. nor listed in the militia aforesaid, who " are now possessed of any gun, powder, shot, or any " weapon, offensive or defensive, may sell and dispose " thereof, at any time before the last day of October " next ensuing. And that all Negroes, Mulattos or " *Indians*, bond or free, living at any frontier plan- " tation, be permitted to keep and use guns, powder " and shot, or other weapons, offensive or defensive; " having first obtained a licence for the same, &c." Idem 342. The disarming of men is the greatest badge of Slavery, and there are multitudes of *free Negroes, Indians*, &c. who are not included in the xvth section as *housekeepers*, and cannot therefore have the benefit of this exception.

By the 22d section of the same law, (p. 343.) it is ordained, " That where any female Mulatto or *Indian*, " by law obliged to serve 'till the age of *thirty* or *thirty-* " *one* years, shall, during the time of her servitude, " have any child born of her body, *every such child shall* " *serve* the master or mistress of such Mulatto or *In-* " *dian, until it shall attain* THE SAME AGE *the mother* " *of such child was obliged by law to serve unto.*"

" And the 23d section is equally unjust and oppressive, " That *no free Negro, Mulatto*, or INDIAN *whatsoever*, " shall hereafter have ANY VOTE *at the election* of *bur-* " *gesses, or any other election* whatsoever." Id. p. 344.

An Act of the 17th Charles II. c. viii. sect. ii. concerning the *Indians*, ordains,—" That if any Eng- " lishman be murdered, the next town shall be answer- " able for it, with *their lives or liberties* to the use of " the publick; and that the honourable the Governor

" be humbly requested forthwith to impower such per-
" sons as his Honour *shall think fit*, in each county, " on such occasions, for putting the said law into im- " mediate execution;" &c. (Id. p. 37.) Thus a *free* Indian, howsoever innocent, may be *murdered* or *enslaved* according to this unjust law, for the wickedness of another! nay, not only himself, but also all his relations, friends, and fellow-townsmen, as innocent as himself, and that merely for the single crime of one unknown murderer!

Sect. iii. " And be it further enacted *by this grand* " *assembly*, that the said *Indians* shall not have power, " within themselves, to elect or constitute their own " *Werowance*, or chief commander, but the present ho- " nourable Governor and his successors, from time to " time, shall constitute and authorize such person, in " whose fidelity they may find greatest cause to repose a " confidence, to be the chief commander of the re- " spective towns: and in case the *Indians* shall refuse " their obedience to, or murder such person, then " that nation of Indians, so refusing or offending, to " be accounted enemies and rebels, and to be pro- " ceeded against accordingly." (Id. p. 37.) Thus our American provincials (though they pretend to be very zealous in the cause of liberty, yet) make no scruple to deprive the poor Indians of their just rights, who are as much intitled to an equitable and reasonable freedom as themselves. It is a shame to this nation, and may in time prove very dangerous to it, that the *British* constitution and liberties should be excluded from any part of the *British dominions*; for without these, the several nations of East or West Indians, and the mixt people who live therein, cannot have so true an interest in the *British government*, as to engage their fidelity to it. Besides, it is the grossest infringement on the *King's Prerogative*, that " the *influence, benefit,* " *and protection of the King's laws and courts of justice*" should not be extended " *to all his Majesty's subjects*" of every denomination (Slaves as well as others) even in the remotest parts of the *British empire*. By the present distracted state of Poland, we may learn the great danger of enslaving the common people, and of permitting any particular rank or order of subjects, to ex-

free Negroes, Mulattoes, Indians, and even *free* or indentured white Servants * are bound

ercise a despotic power over their fellow subjects: for no government can be safe, where this kind of vassalage, or undue authority prevails.

* By the laws of Virginia, (4 Ann. c. xlix. sect. vii.) a master who "*shall presume to whip a Christian white* "*servant naked*" without an order from a justice of peace, forfeits no more "for the same," than *forty* "*shillings sterling*, to the party injured." (Id. p. 219.) A very inadequate penalty for so gross an injury! Whereas on the other hand, "if any servant shall *re-* "*sist* the master or mistress, or overseer," (it matters not *how justly*, for there is no exception whatsoever) "or "offer violence to any of them, the said servant shall, "for every such offence, be adjudged to serve his or "her said master or owner, *one whole year* after the "time, by indenture, custom, or former order of "court, shall be expired." (See sect. xiv. id. p. 221.) The value of a whole year's service bears no proportion with the penalty of forty shillings on the master, so that there is certainly a *much greater* penalty laid on the servant for a *much less* offence. The same act indeed ordains, (sect. viii.) "that all servants (*not being Slaves*) "whether imported, or become servants of their own "accord here, or bound by any court or church-war- "dens, shall have their complaints received by a justice "of peace, who, if he find cause, shall bind the mas- "ter over to answer the complaint at court, and it shall "be there determined; and all complaints of servants "shall and may, by virtue hereof, be received at any "time, upon petition, in the court of the county "wherein they reside, without the formal process of "an action; and also full power and authority is hereby "given to the said court, by their discretion, (having "first summoned the masters *or* OWNERS, (as they un- "justly call them) to justify themselves, *if they think* "*fit*) to adjudge, order and appoint, what shall be "necessary, as to diet, lodging, clothing, and *cor-* "*rection*; and if any master or OWNER shall not there- "upon

" upon *comply* with the ſaid court's order," (now I defy any man in this kingdom, who has not read theſe laws, to gueſs what follows, I mean, what kind of *relief* the injured party is entitled to! One would naturally expect that the maſter ſhould be liable to ſome very ſevere penalty, ſuch as men deſerve who grind the face of the poor; or that the *injured* ſervant ſhould be diſcharged from all obligation of ſervice for the remaining term of his contract, in order to make him ſome amends for his ſufferings, but then a reaſonable *relief* of this kind would not be at all agreeable to the uſual *inconſiſtency* and *injuſtice* of laws enacted by Slaveholders, and therefore) " the ſaid court is hereby (continues the act) au-" thorized and impowered, upon a *ſecond* JUST COM-" PLAINT, to order ſuch ſervant to be immediately " SOLD *at an outcry*, by the Sheriff, and after charges " deducted, the remainder of what the ſaid ſervant " ſhall be SOLD FOR, to be paid and ſatisfied TO SUCH " OWNER."—So that the *owner* (as he is unjuſtly called) is abſolutely to be paid for his vile and ſcandalous oppreſſion, inſtead of being puniſhed for it! " Pro-" vided always" (ſays the following ſection ix.) " and " be it enacted, that if *ſuch* Servant" (ſuch as are ſpoken of in the preceding ſection, including " *all Ser-" vants, not being Slaves*", according to the expreſs words of the Act) " be ſo ſick or lame, or otherwiſe " rendered ſo uncapable, that he or ſhe cannot be *ſold* " for ſuch a value, at leaſt, as ſhall ſatisfy the fees, " and other incidents accrued, the ſaid court ſhall then " order the churchwardens of the pariſh to take care " of and provide for the *ſaid Servant,* until *ſuch Ser-" vant's* time, due by law to the ſaid maſter or *own-" er* ſhall be expired, or until *ſuch Servant*" (now mark the GENEROSITY of theſe lawgivers) " ſhall be " ſo recovered, as to *be ſold* for defraying the ſaid " fees and charges:" A new method this (but not very Chriſtian-like) to reimburſe the *charitable expence of providing for the ſick and lame.*

In the latter end of the ſame ſection it is ordained, that " the ſaid court, from time to time, ſhall order " the charges of keeping the ſaid Servant, to be le-" vied upon the goods and chattels of the maſter or " owner of the ſaid Servant by diſtreſs." But this can

 " only

only mean, that in case the sick Servant shall *not so recover*, "as to be *sold* for defraying the said fees and "charges," the master shall then be liable to defray the said charges.—But if it means any thing else, I must acknowledge myself incapable of fathoming so profound an inconsistency. It would take up much more room than I have here to spare, were I to recount the various kinds of oppression, to which *free Servants*, both white and black, are obliged to submit in the colonies. Nevertheless, in the "Acts of Assembly passed in the island of Barbadoes" (printed at London, 1732) we find still remaining, the titles of many Acts "TO ENCOURAGE "the bringing of Christian servants," &c. but the 454th Act in the said book will inform us what kind of ENCOURAGEMENT Servants are to expect, howsoever specious the promises may be that are made them. "Where-"as (says this Act) several Christian Servants, lately "brought to this island, UPON THE ENCOURAGEMENT "of an Act dated the 25th of June 1696, and put "upon the public treasurer and the country's account, "are yet unplaced; Be it enacted, &c." Then follow some regulations relating to the placing them in the militia; and afterwards we find the following notable clause of *encouragement*, viz. "That if, after the va-"cancies are filled up, as aforesaid, there *shall remain* "*any of* THE SAID SERVANTS still undisposed of, that "then and in such case (upon his Excellency's war-"rant to the treasurer of this island for so doing) it "shall be lawful for the said treasurer TO SELL and "DISPOSE of SUCH overplus and supernumerary SER-"VANTS *for the public account*, within one and twenty "days after publication of this Act, unto any *person* "*or persons* THAT WILL BUY and GIVE MOST FOR "THEM, the same to be applied to the payment of the "*importers of the said Servants*, and to no other use "whatsoever; any law or custom to the contrary not-"withstanding."

FINE ENCOURAGEMENT this for *Free Christian Servants!*

When a Freeman is thus unwarily enslaved, though it may seem to be only for a limited time, yet his condition becomes almost as uncertain, though not quite so abject and perilous, as that of the poor wretched Negroes,

Negroes, for he will find himſelf, as it were *entangled in Slavery*, by a multitude of arbitrary laws, of which, moſt likely, he had not even the leaſt ſuſpicion beforehand.

Every miſdemeanor (though the moſt natural) is made a pretence to extort ſervitude, and lengthen this unnatural confinement of Servants. "If a Servant "ſhall beget a woman Servant with child, then *after* "*his time is expired*, he ſhall ſerve the owner of the ſaid "woman ſervant *double the time* ſhe had to ſerve at the "time of the offence." Laws of Barbadoes, No. 21. clauſe vii. p. 22.

So that in ſome caſes this penalty may be ſo enormous, as even to include all the prime of a man's life.

Now if *fornication* is thus ſeverely puniſhed, one would naturally ſuppoſe that virtuous Servants, who are inclined to *marry*, might hope for ſome *encouragement*, or at leaſt, *mercy* from the legiſlature; but alas! we ſhall find that theſe laws do not even aim at juſtice, and that reaſon and equity muſt in every caſe give place to the private intereſt of the maſter. "If *any Freeman* "(ſays the 8th clauſe of the ſame act) ſhall marry the "maid or woman Servant of any perſon within this "iſland, ſuch *freeman* ſhall forthwith pay unto the "maſter and owner of ſuch Servant DOUBLE THE "VALUE" (a moſt exorbitant and unjuſt fine!) "of "what the maid or woman Servant is worth, &c."—— "But if he be a Servant, then after his time is ex- "pired, he ſhall ſerve the owner of the ſaid woman "Servant DOUBLE THE TIME ſhe had to ſerve at ſuch "her time of marriage." p. 23.

Thus marriage and fornication, as if *equally* criminal, are *equally* puniſhed, and that beyond all bounds of proportion to the loſs of ſervice, which any maſter can poſſibly ſuſtain *by either act!*

Now if the "*forbidding to marry*" is to be reckoned amongſt "*the doctrine of devils*," (ſee 1 Timothy iv. 1, 3.) to what influence ought we to attribute the dictating of this unnatural and deſtructive law?

One would ſuppoſe, that the *grand enemy of mankind* had likewiſe been concerned in making an act of the aſſembly of Virginia againſt matrimony, (4 Ann, ch. 48. ſect. vi. p. 216.)

" That if any minifter or reader fhall wittingly " publifh, or caufe or fuffer to be publifhed, the banns " of matrimony, between ANY SERVANTS, or between " a free perfon and a Servant; or if any minifter fhall " wittingly celebrate the rites of matrimony between " ANY SUCH, without a certificate from the mafter or " miftrefs of every fuch Servant, that it is done by " their confent, he fhall forfeit and pay *ten thoufand* " *pounds* of tobacco: and every Servant fo married, " without the confent of his or her mafter or miftrefs, " fhall, for his or her SAID OFFENCE, ferve his or her " faid mafter or miftrefs, their executors, &c. one " whole year, after the time of fervice by indenture or " cuftom is expired; and moreover, every perfon be- " ing free, and fo marrying with a Servant, fhall, for " his or her SAID OFFENCE, forfeit and pay to the maf- " ter or owner of fuch Servant, one thoufand pounds " of tobacco, or well and faithfully ferve the faid mafter " &c.—one whole year in actual fervice." But befides thefe natural occurrences occafioned by the mutual love of each fex, there are many other circumftances in the behaviour of Servants, which thefe iniquitous laws lay hold of to *entrap* and extort involuntary fervice.

" Whatfoever Servant or Servants fhall wilfully and " obftinately abfent himfelf out of his or her mafter's " or miftrefs's plantation or fervice, either on SATUR- " DAY, SUNDAY, or any other days or times, not " having *licence* or *ticket* in writing, &c.——fhall for " every two hours abfence, &c.—ferve his faid mafter " or miftrefs, *one whole day*, after his time by inden- " ture or cuftom is expired; fo that the fame do not, " in the whole, exceed three years, &c." (Laws of Barbadoes, Act xxi. claufe x. p. 23.)

Now (as in this cafe, one whole day muft be reckoned to include a day and a night) it muft appear, that a Servant in Barbadoes, is unjuftly compelled to make good every lofs of time TWELVE FOLD; which is an abominable ufury!

By the fame act, " in cafe any Servant or Servants " in this ifland" (fee provifo to 11th claufe) " fhall " through their own wilful mifbehaviour happen to have " any difeafe, or any broken bones, bruifes, or other im- " pediments, whereby they have not only difabled them-

" felves

" ſelves to perform their labour as they ought to do,
" but alſo are a greater charge for phyſick and chirur-
" gery to their maſter and miſtreſs than formerly;
" for ſatisfaction of ſuch maſter or miſtreſs in every
" ſuch caſe, the ſaid Servant ſhall ſerve his or her ſaid
" maſter or miſtreſs, after the time by indenture or
" otherwiſe is expired, until they have made ſatisfaction
" for the charges expended on them for their recovery.
" And afterwards he or ſhe hath ſo recovered, ſhall
" ſerve over ſo much time as he or ſhe, by any ſuch
" means and accident, were diſabled to ſerve; any
" thing formerly provided to the contrary notwith-
" ſtanding."

A moſt uncharitable clauſe! That the rich land-holder may not be obliged, even for the furtherance of his own ſervice, to relieve his ſick and maimed ſervants at *his own expence*, the law gives him full power to extort a future involuntary recompence from the bones of the unfortunate ſufferer!

Is not this to "*grind the faces of the poor?*" (ſee Iſaiah iii. 15. and the judgments denounced thereupon.)

But the ſlaveholder perhaps will endeavour to excuſe this law, becauſe it includes (ſays he) no ſickneſs, broken bones, &c. but ſuch as are occaſioned by the Servant's "*own wilful miſbehaviour.*"

Nevertheleſs the deceit and injuſtice of the clauſe is too apparent to be ſcreened by any excuſe whatſoever, for it was manifeſtly calculated to oppreſs and extort ſervitude through the partial conſtruction which may too eaſily be put upon every kind of accident or diſorder.

Suppoſe, for inſtance, that the ſickneſs, broken bones, bruiſes, &c. are occaſioned even by the cruelty of the maſter, or by the ſervant's attempt to eſcape and avoid the ſame, yet ſuch a maſter will readily alledge the Servant's "*wilful miſbehaviour,*" which firſt provoked his ſeverity.

In ſhort, it is much more eaſy for an avaritious maſter to attribute any accident or diſorder to "*wilful* "*miſbehaviour,*" and to ſupport ſuch a charge before a plantation juſtice, (who inherits the ſame prejudices as himſelf, and has a ſimilar intereſt to maintain,) than for

for a poor friendlefs Servant to difprove the charge, howfoever unjuft.

And if the latter in fuch cafe fhould feek for redrefs from a court of juftice, and not be able to produce fuch undeniable evidence, that even partiality itfelf could not for fhame reject it, (for fuch only he muft expect will be admitted by a jury of planters) he might have the mortification to find (like a fly in a cobweb) that all his endeavours to difengage himfelf, would ferve only to entangle him the more, by affording a further occafion for his ungenerous mafter to prolong his Servitude. For by the 18th claufe of the fame act it is ordained, "That what Servants fhall fo unjuftly trouble his mafter or miftrefs *with fuits in law*, the faid Servant fhall be, by the court where he commits the offence, ordered to ferve his mafter or miftrefs *fo injured*, for his unlawful and unjuft vexation of them" (for fo be fure they will efteem it, if the Servant cannot bring fuch proofs as are before-mentioned) "after the expiration of the time he hath then to ferve, the *double term and fpace of that time* he neglected." And the 19th claufe ordains, "That all fuch Servants as fhall be in the gaol for their own offences, fhall ferve their mafters DOUBLE SO LONG TIME after the expiration of the time they have to ferve by cuftom, indenture or contract, as he or they have lain in gaol for fuch their offences, as aforefaid; and fhall further ferve his or her faid mafter, after the RATE OF ONE HUNDRED POUNDS OF SUGAR PER MONTH, till he hath fatisfied their fees and other charges his mafter hath expended on him." Thus a Servant, when his Service is eftimated for the advantage of the mafter, is obliged to make fatisfaction after the rate of one hundred pounds of fugar per month; but when the fatisfaction is to be made to himfelf for the *fame* fervice, as his own juft due for wages, his fervice for even five years, though he be above eighteen years of age, (fee act 21. claufe 16.) is rated only at four hundred pounds of Mufcovadoe fugar, which is *merely one fifteenth part* of the former rate. A moft iniquitous partiality! But the greateft hardfhip of all others is, that they are not permitted to leave the colony without a licence: and as it appears that pretences are

are ſo eaſily made for the refuſal of a diſcharge, they remain entirely at the mercy of the plantation tyrants, and are obliged to accept of ſuch miſerable wages and allowances, as the latter ſhall think proper to give them, either by indenture or otherwiſe. Maſters of ſhips are bound by oath, that they "will not know-"ingly or willingly carry, &c. ANY SERVANT or "Slave, that is not attending his or her maſter, or "ſent by ſuch maſter or owner." (ſee laws of Virginia, p. 370. 12 Geo. I. c. iv. ſect. 18.) And by an act of 4 Ann, c. xii. ſect. 2. p. 147. "No maſter of "a ſhip, ſloop, boat, or other veſſel, ſhall tranſport or "carry ANY SERVANT WHATSOEVER, &c." without a licence, &c. upon penalty of "fifty pounds for every "Servant, &c." According to a law of Barbadoes, (No. 21. clauſe 23. p. 27.) Every maſter of a ſhip is obliged to give a ſecurity of two thouſand pounds, that he will not carry away "ANY SERVANT OR SLAVE," &c. without the conſent of the owner; and he forfeits this bond, till ſatisfaction be made, if he carries off the iſland "ANY FREEMEN, SERVANTS OR SLAVES," without a ticket for the ſame. (No. 347. p. 132.)

By the 22d clauſe of the 21ſt act, "a Servant by ONLY "ENDEAVOURING to get aboard ſome ſhip, bark, or "boat, to eſcape, &c. ſhall upon conviction thereof, "before ANY ONE of his Majeſty's juſtices of the peace "for this iſland, be *condemned* Servant to his maſter or "miſtreſs, for the full ſpace and term of three years." —after the "firſt indenture or ſervice by cuſtom ſhall "be expired;" and "before the *ſame juſtice*, the ſaid Ser-"vant's hair *to be ſhaved off*." Thus, the liberties of Servants are at the mercy of *any one* juſtice of the peace, who happens to be influenced by their maſters or miſtreſſes, or elſe has a ſimilar intereſt in the oppreſſion of Servants.

But though there is ſuch great difficulty to eſcape from the oppreſſive ſervitude of the plantations, yet the moſt flattering and ſpecious promiſes are made by plantation agents and others, to entice thither poor ignorant Servants and Labourers.—"The laws alſo," (ſays Mr. Godwyn) "which are tranſmitted hither to invite the "ſubjects into thoſe parts, are many of them ſo intri-"cate and obſcure, (not to ſay contradictory and falla-

"cious)

" cious) that they ſeem rather to be *traps* and *pit-falls*, " than laws: I ſhall inſtance in two. The firſt is, " that wherein ſervitude for four years is made the " penalty of accepting of another's kindneſs (if I may " ſo term it;) that is, for permitting one's ſelf to be " tranſported *gratis*, when with much ſeeming curteſie " and importunity offered unto them: for thereby the " party (whether miniſter or other, without exception) " doth, by virtue of that law, put himſelf into the " tranſporter's power, and is made to become his Ser- " vant, or to ranſom himſelf from that thraldom and " miſery at a very great rate, perhaps *four or five times* " *ſo much as their paſſage ſhould have coſt them.* A deceit " which no *Engliſhman*, not verſed in thoſe *American* " *arts* and *frauds*, can provide againſt; and is indeed " the great ſtay and ſupport of the *kidnapper's trade* " *and myſtery.* A *trade* that, it is thought, carries off " and conſumes not ſo little as ten thouſand people out " of this kingdom yearly; which might have been a " defence to their mother country, but now are many " of them miſerably deſtroyed, without any advantage " to it." (See the Negroes and Indian's Advocate, ſuing for their Admiſſion into the Church, &c. by Morgan Godwyn, London 1680, pages 170 and 171.) The laws of Virginia, indeed, profeſs to diſcountenance "*the kidnapper's trade*," yet ſo trifling and inſignificant is the penalty againſt it, that this heinous crime ſeems rather to receive a ſanction by law, (ſince the law makes ſo light of it) than a prohibition.

The act to which I refer is the 4 Anne, cap. xlix. ſect. v. p. 219.—" That if any perſon or perſons ſhall here- " after import into this colony, and here ſell as a Slave, " any perſon or perſons that ſhall have been A FREE- " MAN IN ANY CHRISTIAN COUNTRY, ISLAND, OR " PLANTATION, ſuch importer and ſeller as aforeſaid, " ſhall forfeit and pay, TO THE PARTY FROM WHOM " THE SAID FREEMAN SHALL RECOVER HIS FREE- " DOM, double the ſum for which the ſaid freeman " was ſold, &c."——Now ſuppoſe for example ſake, that a kidnapper ſhould *rob* one hundred poor unwary natives of Great Britain or Ireland *of their liberties*, and ſhould afterwards be even abſolutely *convicted* of ſtealing or trepanning no leſs than fifty of them, yet he may

" be

be ſaid to ſtand clear of all puniſhment by this (I think I may very juſtly ſay with Mr. Godwyn) "*contradictory and fallacious*" law: becauſe the wages of his iniquity, in rendering one hundred poor men miſerable, will be ſufficient to inſure him from loſs, even though ſo large a proportion *as half of them*, ſhould afterwards find friends (which indeed is very improbable) or opportunity to enable them to *prove* the injury, and convict the offender; and whatever ſucceſs the ſaid offender may happen to have *above this proportion*, the ſame will be *all clear gain*, without his running the leaſt riſk of *corporal* puniſhment, (I mean in this world) any more than if he had dealt in fair merchandize.

The iniquity of this law will appear ſtill more glaring, if we conſider, that the penalty is not to be paid to the *injured* perſon, but "*to the party from whom the ſaid* "*freeman ſhall recover his freedom*;" that is, in other words, TO THE KIDNAPPER'S ACCOMPLICE, who bought the ſaid freeman; for *the receiver* (as in the caſe of *ſtolen goods* in England. See 3 and 4 William and Mary, ch. ix. and 5 Anne ch. 31.) may undoubtedly be accounted "ACCESSARY" to the crime.

The preamble to one of the laws of Barbadoes, (No. 139. p. 72. London Edition, 1732.) bears ſufficient teſtimony of the horrid practices againſt the liberties of free Servants, as alſo of other "*artificers and ſmall ſettlers*," and of the poſſibility of ſuch perſon's being held in an unjuſt Slavery in other colonies; yet the ſaid law ordains no condign puniſhment for ſuch heinous offences, neither is there any probable remedy propoſed therein for the relief of the much injured Servant, &c. There is indeed a fine of 4000 lbs. of ſugar laid upon thoſe perſons "*who ſhall bargain, contract, or agree to* "*carry off* (that) *iſland any perſon or perſons to ſerve for* "*time*;" but the ſame is not made payable by way of damages to the Servant or Artificer, who finds himſelf *deceived* or *injured* by ſuch a bargain, but only "*the one-* "*half to him that ſhall inform for the ſame, and the other* "*half to the uſe of* (that) *iſland*." Thus it is plain, that the law makers concerned themſelves no farther in preventing ſuch groſs abuſes, than they thought the ſame might be liable to affect their own private intereſt, by the decreaſe of Servants in that iſland.

A former

bound and held, without any probability of relief, we need not doubt, but that the greateſt part of thoſe, who had before been tolerably well uſed in their maſter's family, would be willing, for the ſake of a cer-

A former act (No. 21.) contains, indeed, a clauſe "againſt bringing Servants againſt their wills," (ſee clauſe ii. p. 21.) which allows Servants "liberty to im-"plead the perſons who brought them, or to whom they "are conſigned according to the laws of England, for "their freedom, and to recover damages and ſatisfac-"tion for ſuch injurious dealing." But the injured party cannot be benefited by this clauſe, unleſs "his or "her complaint" is made "to ſome juſtice of the "peace, within THIRTY DAYS after his or her land-"ing in this iſland, unleſs they be prevented by *ſick-"neſs*, and then within thirty days after he or ſhe is "able." So that however merciful this clauſe may ſeem at firſt ſight, yet it is certainly deſtitute of the ſpirit of the Engliſh law, wherein no leſs a time than *two years* is thought neceſſary to be allowed for the commencement of ſuch complaint. (See Habeas Corpus Act, ſect. 17.) For there are many other accidents and impediments, beſides *ſickneſs*, (the only exception allowed in this law of Barbadoes) which might prevent the ſeeking of redreſs in ſo ſhort a time as *thirty days*; ſo that a poor unhappy Servant may, by this very clauſe, without any fault of his own, be for ever excluded from the rights of a free-born Engliſhman.

My ſmall ſhare of leiſure will not permit me to be certain, that there are no other laws better calculated for the relief of Servants in ſuch caſes, than the laſt mentioned clauſe; nevertheleſs, if we conſider the ſpirit of the ſeveral laws which I have already quoted, we may eaſily gueſs what kind of redreſs poor oppreſſed Servants and Artificers are likely to obtain from ſuch ſelf-intereſted diſpenſers of law, as the plantation law-makers.

tain

tain livelihood, to *contract* themſelves again to the ſame maſter, or, at leaſt it is probable, that they would be willing to do ſo upon reaſonable and limited terms, ſuch as might render their condition leſs precarious than the abject and miſerable ſtate to which they were formerly *liable* (howſoever indulgent their reſpective maſters might have been to them) through the arbitrary, cruel and inhuman * ſpirit of plantation legiſlators. And when this precaution of a written agreement is taken, the indentured Slaves will indeed remain the private property of their maſters for the term of their contracts, even in England, (as I have before remarked) and the maſters "*may legally compel them to return again to the plantations*" by virtue of the xiiith ſect. of the Habeas Corpus act, provided that they do not *unlawfully* confine or hurt their perſons. (See part I. p. 10.)

* According to the laws of Jamaica, printed at London in 1756, "if any Slave, having been one whole "year in this iſland, (ſays an act No. 64. clauſe v. p. "114.) ſhall run away, and continue abſent from his "owner's ſervice for the ſpace of thirty days, upon "complaint and proof, &c. before *any two* juſtices of "the peace, and three freeholders, &c. it ſhall and "may be lawful for ſuch juſtices and freeholders, to "order ſuch Slave to be puniſhed by CUTTING OFF "ONE OF THE FEET OF SUCH SLAVE, or inflicting "ſuch other corporal puniſhment as they SHALL THINK "FIT."

"FIT." Now that I may inform my readers what corporal punishments are sometimes THOUGHT FIT to be inflicted, I will refer to the testimony of Sir Hans Sloane. (See Voyage to the island of Madera, Barbadoes, Nieves, St. Christophers, and Jamaica, with the natural History of the last of these Islands, &c. London 1707. Introduction, p. 56 and 57.) "The punish-"ments for crimes of Slaves, (says he) are usually *for* "*rebellions* burning them, by nailing them down on "the ground with crooked sticks on every limb, and "then applying the fire by degrees from the feet and "hands, burning them gradually up to the head, "whereby THEIR PAINS ARE EXTRAVAGANT. For "crimes of a lesser nature, *gelding, or chopping off half* "*of the foot* with an axe. These punishments are suf-"fered by them with great constancy.—For running "away, they put iron rings of great weight on their "ankles, or pottocks about their necks, which are "iron rings with two long necks rivetted to them, or "a spur in the mouth.

"For negligence, they are usually whipped by "the overseers with lance wood switches, till they be "bloody, and several of the switches broken, being "first tied up by their hands in the mill houses. Beat-"ing with manati straps is thought too cruel, and "therefore prohibited by the customs of the country. "The cicatrices are visible on their skins forever after; "and a Slave, the more he have of those, is the less "valued. After they are whipped till *they are raw*, "some *put on their skins pepper and salt* to make them "smart; at other times their masters *will drop melted wax* "*on their skins*, and use several VERY EXQUISITE "TORMENTS. These punishments are sometimes "merited by the Blacks, who are a very perverse gene-"ration of people, and though they appear harsh, yet are "scarce equal to some of their crimes, and inferior to "what punishments other European nations inflict on "their Slaves in the East Indies, as may be seen by "Moquet, and other travellers." Thus Sir Hans Sloane endeavours to excuse those shocking cruelties; but certainly in vain: because no crimes whatsoever can *merit* such severe punishment, unless I except the crimes of those who devise and inflict them. Sir Hans Sloane,

Sloane, indeed, mentions *rebellion* as the principal crime, and certainly it is very justly esteemed a most heinous crime in a land of liberty, where government is limited by equitable and just laws, if the same are *tolerably* well observed; but in countries where arbitrary power is exercised with such *intolerable* cruelty, as is before described, if resistance be a crime, it is certainly the most natural of all others.

But the 19th clause of the 38th act, would, indeed, on a slight perusal, induce us to conceive, that the punishment for *rebellion* is not so severe as it is represented by Sir Hans Sloane; because a Slave, though "DEEMED REBELLIOUS," is thereby condemned to no greater punishment than *transportation*. Neverthelefs, if the clause be thoroughly considered, we shall find no reason to commend the mercy of the legislature: for it only proves, that the Jamaica law-makers will not scruple to charge the slightest and most natural offences with the most opprobrious epithets; and that a poor Slave, who perhaps has no otherwise incurred his master's displeasure, than by endeavouring (upon the just and warrantable principle of self-preservation) to escape from his master's tyranny, without any criminal intention whatsoever, is liable to be DEEMED REBELLIOUS, and to be arraigned as a capital offender. For "every "Slave and Slaves that shall run away, and continue "but for the space of twelvemonths, except such Slave "or Slaves as shall not have been three years in this "island, shall *be deemed* REBELLIOUS, &c." (See act xxxviii. clause xix. p. 60.) Thus we are enabled to define, what a West Indian tyrant means by the word REBELLIOUS. But unjust as this clause may seem, yet it is abundantly more merciful and considerate than a subsequent act, against the same poor miserable people, because the former assigns no other punishment for persons so DEEMED REBELLIOUS, than that they "*shall* "*be transported by order of two justices and three freehold-* "*ers, &c.*" whereas the latter spares not the blood of these poor injured fugitives.

For by the 66th act, a reward of 50 l. is offered to those who "shall kill or bring in alive any *rebellious* "*Slave*;" that is, any of these unfortunate people, whom the law has "*deemed rebellious*," as above: and this premium is not only tendered to commiſſioned parties, (ſee 2d clauſe) but even to any private "*hun-" "ter, Slave, or other perſon*" (ſee 3d clauſe). Thus it is manifeſt, that the law treats theſe poor unhappy men with as little ceremony and conſideration, as if they were merely wild beaſts. But the innocent blood that is ſhed in conſequence of ſuch a deteſtable law, muſt certainly call for vengeance on the murderous abettors and actors of ſuch deliberate wickedneſs! And though many of the guilty wretches ſhould even be ſo hardened and abandoned, as never afterwards to be capable of *ſincere* remorſe, yet a time will undoubtedly come, when they will ſhudder with dreadful apprehenſions, on account of the inſufficiency of ſo wretched an excuſe, as that their poor murdered bretheren were by law "*deemed rebellious!*" But bad as theſe laws are, yet, in juſtice to the freeholders of Jamaica, I muſt acknowledge, that their laws are not near ſo cruel and inhuman, as the laws of Barbadoes and Virginia, and ſeem, at preſent, to be much more reaſonable than they have formerly been, many very oppreſſive laws being now expired, and others leſs ſevere, enacted in their room. The cruel clauſe (viz. 33d of the 38th Act) whereby "freed Slaves were to be tried as other Slaves for all "offences capital or criminal," is repealed by the 153d Act. (clauſe 3.) No Slave can now be diſmembered at the will of his owner, under the penalty of one hundred pounds, by the 4th clauſe of the 64th Act. And the wilful murder of a Slave is, by the 183d Act, made felony (though with benefit of the clergy;) and is puniſhed by impriſonment, (ſee clauſe 1.) and the ſecond offence by death, (ſee clauſe 3, &c.)

But it is far otherwiſe in Barbadoes; for by the 329th Act, p. 125, "If any Negro or other Slave, "under puniſhment by his maſter, or his order, for "running away, or any other crimes or miſdemeanors "towards his ſaid maſter, unfortunately ſhall ſuffer in "life or member, which ſeldom happens," (but it is plain by this law that it does ſometimes happen) "*no* "*perſon whatſoever ſhall be liable to any fine therefore:* But "if any man ſhall, OF WANTONNESS, or ONLY OF "BLOODY-MINDEDNESS, or CRUEL INTENTION, "WILFULLY KILL A NEGRO or OTHER SLAVE of

"HIS

" HIS OWN"—(Now the reader, to be ſure, will naturally expect, that ſome very ſevere puniſhment muſt in this caſe be ordained, to deter the *wanton*, *bloody-minded*, *and cruel* wretch from *wilfully killing* his fellow creatures; but alas! the Barbadian law-makers have been ſo far from intending to curb ſuch abandoned wickedneſs, that they have abſolutely made this law, on purpoſe to ſkreen theſe enormous crimes from the juſt indignation of any righteous perſon, who might think himſelf bound in duty to proſecute a *bloody-minded* villain: they have, therefore, preſumptuouſly taken upon them to give a ſanction, as it were by law, to the horrid crime of *wilful murder*; and have accordingly ordained, that he who is guilty of it in Barbadoes, though the act ſhould be attended with all the aggravating circumſtances before-mentioned) " ſhall pay into the public treaſury" (no more than) " FIFTEEN POUNDS STERLING; but " if he ſhall ſo kill another man's, he ſhall pay to the " owner of the Negro, *double the value*, and into the " public treaſury, TWENTY-FIVE POUNDS STERLING; " and he ſhall further, by the next juſtice of the peace, " be bound to his good behaviour, during the plea-" ſure of the governor and council, AND NOT BE " LIABLE TO ANY OTHER PUNISHMENT OR FORFEI-" TURE FOR THE SAME, &c."

The moſt conſummate wickedneſs, I ſuppoſe, that any body of people, under the ſpecious form of a legiſlature, were ever guilty of!

This ſame Act contains ſeveral other clauſes which are ſhocking to humanity, though too tedious to mention here.

According to an Act of Virginia, (4 Anne ch. xlix. ſect. xxxvii. p. 227.) after proclamation is iſſued againſt Slaves that " run away and lie out" it is " lawful for " any perſons whatſoever, TO KILL AND DESTROY " ſuch Slaves by SUCH WAYS AND MEANS, as he, ſhe, " or they SHALL THINK FIT, without accuſation or " impeachment of any crime for the ſame, &c." And leſt *private* intereſt ſhould incline the planter to mercy, (to which we muſt ſuppoſe ſuch people can have no other inducement) it is provided and enacted in the ſucceeding clauſe (No. 38.) " That for *every Slave* " *killed*, in purſuance of this Act, or *put to death by*

 " *law*,

" *law*, the maſter or owner of ſuch Slave *ſhall be paid* " *by the public.*"

Alſo, by an Act of Virginia (9 Geo. I. ch. iv. ſect. xviii. p. 343.) it is ordained, " That, where any " Slaves ſhall hereafter be found notoriouſly guilty of " going abroad in the night, or running away, and " lying out, and cannot be reclaimed from SUCH diſ- " orderly courſes, by the common method of puniſh- " ment, it ſhall and may be lawful, to and for the " court of the county, upon complaint and proof " thereof to them made, by the owner of ſuch Slave, " to order and direct every *ſuch* Slave to be puniſhed, " by DISMEMBERING OR ANY OTHER WAY, not " touching life, as the ſaid county court SHALL THINK " FIT."

I have already given examples enough of the horrid cruelties which are ſometimes THOUGHT FIT, on ſuch occaſions. But if the innocent, and moſt natural act of " *running away*" from intolerable tyranny, deſerves ſuch relentleſs ſeverity, what kind of puniſhment have theſe law-makers themſelves to expect hereafter, on account of their own enormous offences! Alas! to look for mercy (without a timely repentance) will only be another inſtance of their groſs injuſtice! " *Having their conſciences ſeared with a hot iron,*" they ſeem to have loſt all apprehenſion, that their Slaves are men, for they ſcruple not to number them with beaſts.

See an Act of Barbadoes, (No. 333. p. 128.) intitled, " an Act for the better regulating of OUTCRIES " in open market:" here we read of " NEGROES, " CATTLE, COPPERS AND STILLS, AND OTHER " CHATTELS, *brought by execution to open market, to be* " *outcried*;" and theſe (as if all of equal importance) are ranged together, " *in great lots or numbers to be* " *ſold.*"

This unnatural inventory " OF NEGROES, CATTLE, " COPPERS AND STILLS, AND OTHER GOODS OR " CHATTELS" is repeated, nearly in the ſame words, no leſs than ſix times in the 1ſt clauſe. Alſo, " the " marſhal is hereby required" (ſays the ſame clauſe) " to diſpoſe *the Negroes* and *other chattels aforeſaid, into* " *lots*, not exceeding the number of FIVE NEGROES " IN ONE LOT, unleſs it happen that there be more

" than

" than five of one family of Negroes; in which case, " it shall be lawful for the marshal TO SELL A WHOLE " FAMILY IN ONE LOT; and also the marshal is " hereby required not to SELL above FIVE HEAD OF " CATTLE, and *one copper*, or *one still in one lot*, &c."

Thus it too plainly appears, that the Barbadians rank their Negroes with their beasts, so that we need not be surprized, that the former of these are no more instructed in religion, than the latter. But this abominable insult to human nature, bad as it is, yet is not half so criminal, as the deliberate and arbitrary attempt of the assembly at Barbadoes, under the name and sanction of law, to deter others from affording that instruction, which they themselves so uncharitably deny.

The law to which I refer, is the 198th Act, p. 94, intitled, " an Act to prevent people called Qua- " kers, from bringing Negroes to their meetings."

The preamble is as follows:—" Whereas of late, " *many* Negroes have been suffered to remain at the " meeting of Quakers, as hearers of their doctrine, and " *taught* in their principles, whereby the *safety* of this " island may be *much hazarded*, &c."——But is not the *safety* of the island *more hazarded* by suffering an immense multitude of poor ignorant heathens to remain *uninstructed*, even within the families and plantations of a people who call themselves Christians? And is not this danger, likewise, apparently increased, by the barbarous treatment and inhuman insults, which the former daily receive from these nominal Christians, insomuch, that they must necessarily detest the very name of Christians? So much for the reason of the act.—— I now proceed to the penalties of it. The first clause " ordains, " That if, at any time or times after pub- " lication hereof, any Negro or Negroes be found with " the said people called *Quakers*, at any of their meet- " ings, and as hearers of their preachings, that such " Negro or Negroes, shall be forfeited, &c." And by the second clause it is enacted, " That if such Negro " or Negroes, being at the meetings aforesaid, and doth " NOT belong to any of the persons present at the " same meeting, then may any person or persons bring " an action grounded upon this statute, against ANY of

 " the

" the persons present at the said meetings, at the elec-
" tion of the informer, for the sum of ten pounds
" sterling, for *every Negro and Negroes so present*, as
" aforesaid, and shall recover *ten pounds sterling* for
" EVERY *such Negro and Negroes*, &c."

So that an innocent man, merely by being present at a Quakers meeting, may incur, not only the severe penalty of ten pounds sterling, but of as many ten pounds as there shall happen to be Negroes in the meeting, whether he be concerned in bringing any of them thither or not. And in some cases the fine may be so excessive, that even a substantial Quaker is liable to be ruined by a malicious information.

This act, however, does more honour to the Quakers, than the Barbadians, perhaps, are aware of: for it is certainly a lasting monument of the sincerity of the former, and of the detestable injustice and irreligion of the latter. Though I am sufficiently aware of the enormous errors of the Quakers, having carefully perused most of their principal authors, yet am I convinced, that their charitable endeavours to instruct these poor Slaves to the best of their knowledge and belief, will render them more acceptable to God, than all the other sects of nominal Christians, (howsoever orthodox in profession of faith) who either oppose or neglect the same. Is it not a great aggravation of guilt in the latter, that they profess the knowledge of what is right, and yet behave as if themselves were heathens and barbarians? O! that this examplary charity of the Quakers (howsoever despicable their doctrines appear in many other respects) may provoke to jealousy and amendment those lukewarm Christians, who profess, and dishonour a more orthodox faith: lest the heavy judgements of God should speedily overtake them, or permit them to be reduced, in their turn, to a deplorable servitude under barbarians, as unmerciful as themselves!

" In the 329th act of Barbadoes (p. 122.) it is asserted, that " brutish Slaves, deserve not, for the base-
" ness of their condition, to *be tried by a legal trial of*
" *twelve men of their peers or neighbourhood*, which nei-
" ther truly can be rightly done, as the subjects of
" England are," (yet Slaves also are subjects of Eng-

land, whilst they remain within the British dominions, notwithstanding this insinuation to the contrary) "nor "is execution to be delayed towards them, in case of "such horrid crimes committed, &c."

A similar doctrine is taught in an act of *Virginia*, (9 Geo. I. c. iv. sect. iii. p. 339.) wherein it is ordained, "*that every Slave* committing such offence, as by the "laws ought to be punished by DEATH, or LOSS OF "MEMBER, shall be forthwith committed to the com- "mon gaol of the county, &c.—And that the sheriff "of such county, upon such commitment, shall forth- "with certify the same, with the cause thereof, to the "governor or commander in chief, &c. who is there- "upon desired and impowered to issue a commission of "oyer and terminer, TO SUCH PERSONS AS HE SHALL "THINK FIT: which persons, forthwith after the "receipt of such commission, are impowered and re- "quired to cause the offender to be publicly arraigned "and tried, &c.—*without the solemnity of a jury*, &c." Now let us consider the dangerous tendency of those laws.

As Englishmen, we strenuously contend for this absolute and immutable necessity of trials by juries: but is not the spirit and equity of this old English doctrine entirely lost, if we partially confine that justice to ourselves alone, when we have it in our power to extend it to others? The *natural right of all mankind* must principally justify our insisting upon this necessary privilege in favour of ourselves in particular; and therefore if we do not allow, *that the judgment of an impartial jury is indispensably necessary in all cases whatsoever, wherein the life of a man is depending*, we certainly undermine the equitable force and reason of those laws, by which *we ourselves are protected*, and consequently are unworthy to be esteemed either Christians or Englishmen.

Whatsoever right the members of a provincial assembly may have to enact *bye-laws*, for particular exigences among themselves, yet in so doing, they are certainly bound, in duty to their Sovereign, to observe, most strictly, the fundamental principles of that constitution, which his Majesty is sworn to maintain; for wheresoever the bounds of the British empire are extended, there the Common Law of England must of course take place, and cannot ſafely be ſet aſide by any *private law* whatſoever, becauſe the introduction of an unnatural tyranny muſt neceſſarily endanger the King's dominions. The many alarming inſurrections of Slaves in the ſeveral colonies, are ſufficient proofs of this. The Common Law of England ought therefore to be ſo eſtabliſhed in every province, as to *include* the reſpective *bye-laws* of each province, inſtead of being by them *excluded*, which latter has been too much the caſe.

Every inhabitant of the Britiſh colonies, black as well as white bond as well as free, are undoubtedly *the King's ſubjects*, during their reſidence within the limits of the *King's dominions*, and as ſuch, are entitled to perſonal protection, howſoever bound in ſervice to their reſpective maſters. Therefore, when any of theſe are put to death, "WITHOUT THE SOLEMNITY OF A JURY," I fear that there is too much reaſon to attribute THE GUILT OF MURDER, to every perſon concerned in ordering the ſame, or in conſenting thereto; and all ſuch perſons are certainly reſponſible TO THE KING AND HIS LAWS, *for the loſs of a ſubject*. The horrid iniquity, injuſtice, and dangerous tendency of the ſeveral plantation laws, which I have quoted, are ſo apparent, that it is unneceſſary for me to apologize for the freedom with which I have treated them. If ſuch laws are not abſolutely neceſſary for the government of Slaves, the law-makers muſt unavoidably allow themſelves to be the moſt cruel and abandoned tyrants upon earth, or perhaps, that ever were on earth. On the other hand, if it be ſaid, that it is impoſſible to govern Slaves without ſuch inhuman ſeverity and deteſtable injuſtice, the ſame will certainly be an invincible argument againſt the leaſt toleration of Slavery amongſt Chriſtians; becauſe the temporal profits of the planter or maſter, howſoever lucrative, cannot compenſate the forfeiture of his everlaſting welfare, or (at leaſt I may be allowed to ſay) the apparent danger of ſuch a forfeiture.

Oppreſſion is a moſt grievous crime; and the cries of theſe much injured people (though they are only poor ignorant heathens) will certainly reach to Heaven! The Scriptures (which are the only true foundation of all laws) denounce a tremendous judgment againſt the

But ſuppoſe a Slave ſhould abſolutely refuſe to enter into ſuch *a written agreement*, and yet the ſervice of that Slave, either on account of his known fidelity or capacity, is become ſo neceſſary to the maſter, that he cannot eaſily diſpenſe with it.

the man, who ſhould *offend* even ONE *little one.* "It "were better for him," (even the merciful Saviour of the world hath himſelf declared) "that a millſtone were "hanged about his neck, and he caſt into the ſea, than "that he ſhould *offend* ONE *of theſe little* ones." Luke xvii 2. Who then ſhall attempt to vindicate thoſe inhuman eſtabliſhments of government, under which even our own countrymen ſo grievouſly OFFEND and OPPRESS, (not merely ONE, or a few *little ones*, but) an immenſe multitude of *men*, *women*, *children*, and the *children of their children*, from generation to generation? May it not be ſaid with like juſtice—It were better for the Engliſh nation, that theſe American dominions had never exiſted, or even that they ſhould have been ſunk into the ſea, than that the kingdom of Great Britain, ſhould be loaded with the horrid guilt of tolerating ſuch abominable wickedneſs! In ſhort, if THE KING'S PREROGATIVE is not ſpeedily exerted for *the relief* of his Majeſty's oppreſſed and much injured ſubjects in the Britiſh colonies, (becauſe *to relieve the ſubject* from the oppreſſion of petty tyrants, is the principal uſe of royal prerogative, as well as the principal and moſt natural means of maintaining the ſame) and for the extenſion of the Britiſh conſtitution to the moſt diſtant colonies, whether in the Eaſt or Weſt Indies, it muſt inevitably be allowed, that great ſhare of this *enormous guilt* will certainly reſt on this ſide of the water!

I hope this hint will be taken notice of by thoſe whom it may concern; and that the freedom of it will be excuſed, as from a *loyal and diſintereſted* adviſer.

When-

Whenever this happens to be the caſe, the maſter will be apt to think himſelf much aggrieved by the civil liberty and cuſtom of England, which deprives him of the *conſtrained ſervice* of his uſeful Slave, but for my part, I think it cannot be eſteemed an unreaſonable hardſhip upon the maſter, that he ſhould be obliged to make it the intereſt of ſuch a very uſeful perſon, to ſerve and attend him willingly, though it ſhould be at the expence even of the higheſt rate of Servants wages (beſide the loſs of property by the manumiſſion) "*for the Labourer is worthy of his hire**".

I do not apprehend, that the above ſuppoſed caſe will be very general, but if it ſhould, 'tis certainly better, that ſome hardſhip ſhould lie upon thoſe ſelfiſh maſters, who might be ungenerous enough *to think it a hardſhip*, than that a real and national inconvenience ſhould be felt, by permitting every perſon (without any inconvenience to himſelf) to increaſe the preſent ſtock of black Servants in this king-

* St. Luke x. 7. See alſo Timothy v. 18. "For "the Scripture ſaith, thou ſhalt not muzzle the ox "that treadeth out the corn: and, the labourer is wor-"thy of his reward."

dom,

dom, which is already much too numerous. Therefore, even if there ſhould be really any inconvenience or hardſhip upon the maſter, contrary or different to what I have ſuppoſed, 'tis certainly not to be lamented, becauſe the public good ſeems to require ſome reſtraint of this unnatural increaſe of black ſubjects.

Though the advocates for Slavery ſhould ſet forth their plea of PRIVATE PROPERTY (the only plea they can alledge with any the leaſt appearance of juſtice) in the very beſt light that it is capable of, yet I flatter myſelf, that the foregoing conſiderations will be ſufficient to balance it: becauſe A PRIVATE PROPERTY, *which is unnatural in itſelf, inconvenient* and *hurtful to the public,* and (above all) plainly *contrary to the laws and conſtitutions of this kingdom,* cannot juſtly be otherwiſe eſteemed, *than as* A PRIVATE PROPERTY *in contraband goods,* the forfeiture of which, no good citizen ought to regret.

It cannot reaſonably be alledged, that the ſervice of Slaves is neceſſary in England, whilſt ſo many of our own free fellow-ſubjects want bread.

If the Engliſh labourer is not able, with hard work, to earn more than what will

barely

barely provide him his neceſſary food and coarſe or ragged cloathing, what more can his employer reaſonably deſire of him, even if he were his Slave?

The mere boarding and cloathing of a Slave in England (if human nature is not depreſſed and vilified) will undoubtedly be as expenſive to the maſter, as the wages of Engliſh labourers, if not more ſo; becauſe poor men can generally provide for themſelves at a cheaper rate, and will put up with inconveniencies (when the ſame are voluntary), which would really be oppreſſive, nay, even intolerable, from the hand of another perſon.

But, beſides the neceſſary charges of eating and cloathing, there are other expences over and above, to which the employer of free labourers is not ſubject, viz. the prime coſt, as well as freight of the Slave; Apothecaries and Surgeons Bills on account of ſickneſs and accidents, and a multitude of other unavoidable articles, which muſt be defrayed by the maſter.

Now, though the advocates for Slavery ſhould be obliged to allow this (as I think they muſt) with reſpect to labourers, yet perhaps they will ſtill urge, that there is never-

neverthelefs a confiderable advantage by Slaves, when they are kept as domeftics, becaufe no wages are paid, whereas, free Servants are not only cloathed and boarded at the mafter's expence as well as the others, but receive wages into the bargain.

This reafoning, at firft, feems plaufible; but on the other hand, let us fet off the annual intereft of the Slave's price in part of wages, and then divide the principal fum itfelf into as many portions as the average number of years, that a Slave is ufually capable of being ufeful. Befides this, the uncertainty of health and life, muft be thrown into the fcale, unlefs the expence of infurance upon thefe precarious circumftances be likewife added; otherwife the principal fum itfelf is laid out on a very bad fecurity.

Now when all thefe things are weighed and compared with the common rate of Servants wages, there will not appear to be any great faving in the employing of Slaves; efpecially if it be confidered, that healthy and comely boys and girls, the children of our own free fellow-fubjects may be procured out of any county in this or the neighbouring kingdoms, to ferve as

Ap-

apprentices or ſervants, for ſix or ſeven years or more *, without any wages at all; which ought certainly to be remembered, when the average rate of wages to Servants and labourers is mentioned.

Therefore upon the whole, I think it muſt appear, that the ſervice of Slaves in England, would be quite as expenſive, as that of freemen, and conſequently, that there cannot be any real advantages in a toleration of Slavery in this kingdom; at leaſt, I am not able to point them out, though I have carefully conſidered the ſubject. So much for my firſt propoſition.

I am now to conſider the miſchiefs which a toleration of Slavery would be liable to produce, according to my ſecond propoſition.

The learned Monteſquieu † obſerves,

* "And children of poor perſons may be apprenticed out by the overſeers, with conſent of two juſtices, till twenty-four years of age, to ſuch perſons as are thought fitting; who are alſo compellable to take them: and it is held, that gentlemen of fortune and clergymen, are equally liable with others to ſuch compulſion, &c." Commentaries on the laws of England, by William Blackiſtone, Eſq; 3 edit. vol. I. b. i. ch. xiv. p. 426.

† De L'Eſprit des Loix, liv. xv. ch. i. p. 340. "Il n'eſt pas bon par ſa nature; il n'eſt utile ni au maitre ni à L'Eſclave; à celui-ci parcequ'il ne peut rien faire par vertu; à celui-la parcequ'il contracte avec "ſes

concerning Slavery; that " it is not good " in its nature," that " 'tis neither useful " to the master nor Slave; to this, because " he can do nothing through principle (or " virtue;) to the other, because he con- " tracts with his Slaves all sorts of bad " habits, insensibly accustoms himself to " want all moral virtues whatsoever, and " becomes haughty, hasty, hard-hearted, " passionate, voluptuous and cruel."

I could willingly transcribe, not only the succeeding part of this chapter, as being much to my purpose, but even the whole fifteen following chapters, for the same reason; but as they would be much too long for a quotation, and yet contain nothing superfluous, I must beg to refer my readers to the author himself.

A toleration of Slavery is, in effect, a toleration of inhumanity; for there are wretches in the world, who make no scruple to gain, by wearing out their Slaves with continual labour and a scanty allowance, before they have lived out half their natural days. 'Tis notorious, that this is

" ses Esclaves toutes sortes de mauvaises habitudes, " qu'il s'accoutume insensiblement à manquer à toutes " les vertus morales, qu'il devient fier, prompt, dur, " colére, voluptueux, cruel."

too

too often the caſe, in the unhappy countries where Slavery is tolerated.

See the " account of the European ſettlements in America," Part vi. chap. xi. concerning the " *Miſery of the Negroes.* " *Great waſte of them,*" &c. which informs us, not only of a moſt ſcandalous profanation of the Lord's day, but alſo of another abomination, which muſt be infinitely more heinous in the ſight of God; viz. oppreſſion carried to ſuch exceſs, as to be even deſtructive of the human ſpecies.

At preſent the inhumanity of *conſtrained labour in exceſs* extends no farther in England, than to our beaſts, as poſt and hackney horſes, ſand aſſes, &c.

But thanks to our laws, and not to the general good diſpoſition of maſters, that it is ſo; for the wretch, who is bad enough to maltreat a helpleſs beaſt, would not ſpare his fellow man, if he had him as much in his power.

The maintenance of civil liberty is therefore abſolutely neceſſary to prevent an increaſe of our national guilt, by the addition of the horrid crime of tyranny.

It is not my buſineſs at preſent to examine, how far a toleration of Slavery may be be neceſſary or juſtifiable in the Weſt-Indies. 'Tis ſufficient for my purpoſe, that it is not ſo here. But notwithſtanding, that the plea of neceſſity cannot here be urged, yet this is no reaſon, why an increaſe of the practice is not to be feared.

Our North American colonies afford us a melancholy inſtance to the contrary—for tho' the climate in general is ſo wholeſome and temperate, that it will not authorize this plea of neceſſity for the employment of Slaves, any more than our own, yet the pernicious practice of Slave-holding is become almoſt general in thoſe parts.

At New York, for inſtance, this infringement on civil or domeſtic liberty is become notorious and ſcandalous, notwithſtanding that the political controverſies of the inhabitants are ſtuffed with theatrical bombaſt and ranting expreſſions in praiſe of liberty.

But no panegyrick on this ſubject (howſo ever elegant in itſelf) can be graceful or edifying from the mouth or pen of one of thoſe Provincials; becauſe men, who do not ſcruple to detain others in Slavery, have but a very partial and unjuſt claim to the protection of the laws of liberty: and indeed it too plainly appears, that they have no real regard for liberty, farther than their own private interefts are concerned; and (confequently) that they have fo little deteftation for defpotifm and tyranny, that they do not fcruple to exercife them with the moft unbounded rigour, whenever their caprice excites them, or their private intereft, feems to require an exertion of their power over their miferable Slaves.

Every petty planter, who avails himfelf of the fervice of Slaves, is an arbitrary monarch, or rather a lawlefs Bafha in his own territories, notwithftanding that the imaginary freedom of the province, wherein he refides, may feem to forbid the obfervation.

The *boafted liberty* of our American colonies, therefore, has fo little right to that facred name, that it feems to differ from the arbitrary power of defpotic monarchies only in one circumftance; viz. that it is a *many-headed monfter of tyranny*, which entirely fubverts our moft excellent conftitution; becaufe liberty and flavery are fo oppofite to each other, that they cannot fubfift in the fame community.

" Poli-

" Political liberty * (in mild or well re-
" gulated governments) makes civil liberty
" valuable; and whosoever is deprived of the
" latter, is deprived also of the former."

This observation of the learned Montesquieu, I hope, sufficiently justifies my censure of the Americans, for their notorious violation of civil liberty.

Indeed I don't at present recollect, that I ever read any of the American news-papers, except one, viz. " the New-York " Journal, or the General Advertiser," for Thursday 22d October, 1767, No. 1294. But even this one was sufficient to give me a thorough disgust, not less to their extravagant manner of reasoning in defence of liberty, (Hyperion's letter, to wit) than to their shameless infringement upon it by an open profession and toleration of Slave-holding.

This one news-paper gives notice by advertisement, of no less than *eight different persons* who have escaped from Slavery, or are put up to public sale for that horrid purpose.

* " La Liberté politique" (dans les etats modérés) " y rend precieuse la Liberté civile; et celui qui est privé " de cette derniere est encore privé de l'autre." L'Esprit des Loix, tom. i. liv. xv. ch. xii. p. 353.

That

That I may demonſtrate the indecency of ſuch proceedings in a free country, I ſhall take the liberty of laying ſome of theſe advertiſements before my readers, by way of example.

"To be ſold for want of employment."

"A likely ſtrong active Negro man, "of about 24 years of age, this country "born," *(N. B. a natural born ſubject)* "underſtands moſt of a Baker's trade, and "a good deal of farming buſineſs, and can "do all ſorts of houſe-work; alſo a heal-"thy Negro wench of about 21 years old, "is a tolerable cook, and capable of doing "all ſorts of houſe-work, can be well re-"commended for her honeſty and ſobriety; "ſhe has a female child of nigh 3 years "old, which will be ſold with the wench, "if required, &c."

Here is not the leaſt conſideration or ſcruple of conſcience for the inhumanity of parting *the mother* and *young child.* From the ſtile, one would ſuppoſe the advertiſement to be of no more importance, than if it related merely to the ſale of *a cow* and *her calf*; that *the cow* ſhould be ſold with or without *her calf*, according as the purchaſer ſhould require.

The following extract from Sir Hans Sloane's introduction to his Natural Hiſtory of Jamaica, before quoted, will enable us to form ſome idea of the deep affliction with which the poor Negroes are affected upon ſuch occaſions, and conſequently the groſs inhumanity of this advertiſement will more plainly appear. " The Negroes (ſays he) " are uſually thought to be haters of their " own children, and therefore 'tis believed, " that they ſell and diſpoſe of them to " ſtrangers for money, BUT THIS IS NOT " TRUE, for the Negroes of Guinea being " divided into ſeveral captainſhips, as well " as the Indians of America, have wars, " and beſides thoſe ſlain in battles, many " priſoners are taken, who are ſold for " Slaves, and brought hither. But the " parents here, although their children are " Slaves for ever, YET HAVE SO GREAT " LOVE FOR THEM, that no maſter dare " ſell or give away one of their little-ones, " unleſs they *care not* whether their pa- " rents HANG THEMSELVES OR NO."

But not only Negroes, but even American Indians are detained in the ſame abominable Slavery in our colonies, though there cannot be any reaſonable pretence whatſoever, for holding one of theſe as *private property:* for even if *a written contract* ſhould be produced as a voucher in ſuch a caſe, there would ſtill remain great ſuſpicion, that ſome undue advantage had been taken of the Indians ignorance concerning the nature of ſuch a bond.

" Run away, on Monday the 21ſt in-
" ſtant, from J—n Th——s, Eſq; of Weſt
" Cheſter County, in the province of New
" York, an *Indian Slave,* named Abraham,
" he may have changed his name, about
" 23 years of age, about 5 feet 5 inches
" high, *yellow complexion, long black hair*
" *ſomething curled*; a thick ſet fellow, one
" of his fore teeth in the lower jaw broke
" off, &c. *."

Nay! this licentious and unnatural tyranny is become ſo familiar in our colonies, that they venture ſometimes to advertiſe Slaves, without even deigning to diſtinguiſh their complexion at all, of which

* " If he ſmite out his man ſervant's tooth, or his
" maid ſervant's tooth, he ſhall let him go free for his
" tooth's ſake." Exodus xxi. 27.

See another advertiſement in the ſame news-paper, ſigned by Samuel A. Br—tt of Schenectady, wherein an abſconded Negro is alſo deſcribed by marks of injury, viz. " Has *a ſcar under his right eye,*—and is *without his* " *two foremoſt under teeth,* &c."

the following advertiſement in the ſame paper is a proof.

“ *To be ſold for* NO FAULT, *a very good* “ *Wench*, twenty-two years old; *with a* “ *child* eighteen months old. Enquire of “ the Printer.”

By ſuch a deſcription as this, a trepanned Engliſh woman might be ſold, as well as a Negro or Indian.

Upon the whole, I think, I may with juſtice conclude, that theſe advertiſements diſcover ſuch a ſhameleſs proſtitution and infringement on the common and natural rights of mankind, as may entitle the province where they were publiſhed, to the name of New Barbary, rather than of New York!

But hold! perhaps the Americans may be able, with too much juſtice, to retort this ſevere reflection, and may refer us to news-papers publiſhed even in the free city of London, which contain advertiſements, not leſs diſhonourable than their own. See advertiſement in the Public Ledger of 31 December, 1767.

“ For ſale, A healthy Negro Girl, aged “ about fifteen years, ſpeaks good Engliſh, “ works at her needle, waſhes well, does

 “ houſhold

" houſhold work, and has had the ſmall-
" pox. By J. W. at Mr. M'Auley's, the
" Amſterdam Coffee-houſe, near the Ex-
" change, from twelve till two o'clock
" every day."

Another advertiſement, not long ago, offered a reward for ſtopping a female Slave, who had left her miſtreſs in Hatton-Garden. And in the Gazetteer of 18 April, 1769, appeared a very extraordinary advertiſement, with the following title,

" HORSES, TIM WISKY, and *Black Boy*."

" To be ſold, at the Bull and Gate Inn,
" Holborn, a very good Tim Wiſky, little
" the worſe for wear, &c." afterwards,
" *a Cheſnut Gelding*,"——then, " *a very*
" *good Grey Mare*,"——and laſt of all, (as if of the leaſt conſequence) " *a well made*,
" *good-tempered Black Boy*; he has lately
" had the ſmall-pox, and will be ſold to
" any Gentleman. Enquire as above."

Another advertiſement in the ſame paper contains a very particular deſcription of " a
" Negro man, called Jeremiah or Jerry
" Rowland,"—and concludes as follows—
" whoever delivers him to Capt. M-ll-y,
" on board the Elizabeth, at Prince's Stairs,

" Ro-

" Rotherhithe, on or before the 31ſt in-
" ſtant, ſhall receive *thirty guineas reward*,
" or *ten guineas* for ſuch intelligence as
" ſhall enable the captain or his maſter" (Patrick B—rke, Eſq; mentioned above) " effectually to ſecure him. The utmoſt " ſecrecy may be depended on." It is not on account of *ſhame*, that men, *who are capable of undertaking* the deſperate and wicked employment of kidnappers, are ſuppoſed to be tempted to ſuch a buſineſs, by a promiſe of " *the utmoſt ſecrecy*," but this muſt be from a *ſenſe* of the *unlawfulneſs of the act* propoſed to them, that they may have leſs reaſon to fear a proſecution. And as ſuch kind of people are ſuppoſed to undertake any thing for money, the reward of thirty guineas was tendered at the top of the advertiſement in capital letters. No man can be ſafe, be he *white* or black, if *temptations to break the laws* are ſo ſhamefully publiſhed in our news-papers.

" A Creole Black Boy" is alſo offered to ſale, in the Daily Advertiſer of the ſame date.

Beſides theſe inſtances, the Americans may perhaps taunt us with the ſhameful treatment of a poor Negro ſervant, who

not

not long ago was put up to ſale by public auction, together with the effects of his bankrupt maſter.

Alſo that the priſons of this free city have been frequently proſtituted of late by the tyrannical and dangerous practice of confining Negroes, under the pretence of Slavery, though there has been no Warrants whatſoever for their commitment.

This circumſtance of confining a man without a warrant, has ſo great a reſemblance to the proceedings of a Popiſh Inquiſition, that it is but too obvious what dangerous practices ſuch ſcandalous innovations (if permitted to grow more into uſe) are liable to introduce.

No perſon can be ſafe, if wicked and deſigning men have it in their power, under the pretence of private property as a Slave, to throw a man clandeſtinely without a warrant into goal, and to conceal him there, until they can conveniently diſpoſe of him.

A freeman may be thus robbed of his liberty and carried beyond the ſeas, without having the leaſt opportunity of making his caſe known; which ſhould teach us how jealous we ought to be of all impriſonments made without the authority or previous examination of the civil magiſtrate.

The diſtinction of colour will, in a ſhort time, be no protection againſt ſuch outrages, eſpecially as not only Negroes, but Mulattos, and even *American Indians*, (which appears by one of the advertiſements before quoted) are retained in Slavery in our American colonies; for there are many honeſt weather-beaten Engliſhmen, who have as little reaſon to boaſt of their complexion as the Indians. And indeed the more northern Indians have no difference from us in complexion, but ſuch as is occaſioned by the climate or different way of living. The plea of *private* property, therefore, cannot by any means juſtify a *private* commitment of any perſon whatſoever to priſon, becauſe of the apparent danger and tendency of ſuch an innovation.

This dangerous practice of concealing in priſon, was attempted in the caſe of Jonathan Strong; for the door keeper of the P—lt—y C—pt—r (or ſome perſon who acted for him) abſolutely refuſed for two days to permit this poor injured Negro to be ſeen or ſpoke with, though a perſon went on purpoſe both thoſe days to demand the ſame.

How-

However, in excuſe for the Londoners, I have the ſatisfaction to obſerve, that the practice of Slave-holding is now only in its infancy amongſt us; and Slaves are at preſent employed in no other capacity, than that of Domeſtic Servants. But if ſuch practices are permitted much longer with impunity, *the evil will take root*; *precedent and cuſtom will too ſoon be pleaded in its behalf*; and as Slavery becomes more familiar in our eyes, mercenary and ſelfiſh men may take it into their heads, to employ their Slaves (not merely in domeſtick affairs as at preſent, but) in huſbandry; ſo that they may think it worth their while to breed them like cattle on their eſtates, as they do even in the North American colonies, though the children of Slaves, born there, are as much the King's natural born ſubjects as the free natives of England.

God forbid that this ſhould ever be the caſe here! However, we cannot be too jealous of every thing that tends to it; leſt it ſhould afterwards be remarked, that a *miſunderſtanding, or miſtaken opinion of the lawyers of this age*, has introduced a vaſſalage much more diſgraceful and pernicious, than that which the *ancient lawyers* have ſo happily aboliſhed.

This

This is not altogether a chimera. A difpofition, howfoever impolitic and unnatural, which prevails in one place, may prevail likewife in another.

The account of the American fettlements before quoted, informs us (in vol. ii. p. 117.) of a certain unnatural difpofition of the planters, "*to do every thing by Negroes, which can poffibly be done by them,*" notwithftanding that there are wholefome laws to oblige them to keep a certain proportion of white Servants: and the ingenious author obferves thereupon, that, "*if this dif-*" "*pofition continues, in a little time (which is*" "*indeed nearly the cafe already), all the*" "*Englifh in our colonies there will con-*" "*fift of little more than a few planters*" "*and merchants; and the reft will be a*" "*defpicable, though a dangerous, becaufe a*" "*numerous and difaffected, herd of African*" "*Slaves.*" Id. p. 118.

It would indeed be abfurd to conceive, that fuch a difpofition can very foon become general here in England, yet there is no abfurdity in fuppofing a poffibility of its being introduced by flow degrees.

A very

A very learned and reſpectable author (whoſe performance * in other reſpects I admire and eſteem) has dropped ſome hints concerning Slavery, which at firſt ſight may ſeem to favour the arguments of thoſe who contend for the introduction of it here, and who endeavour to juſtify the modern unnatural claims of *private property* in the perſons of men: but with reſpect to the author himſelf, indeed, it is plain he had no ſuch views, he having only introduced the topic of Slavery, in order to prove a very different point, in which he certainly ſucceeds. Nay, he himſelf declares againſt any ſuch intentions.—" God " forbid, (ſays he in p. 91.) that I ſhould " ever be an advocate for Slavery, eccle- " ſiaſtic, civil or domeſtic, on account of " any accidental advantages, which it may

* " A Diſſertation on the Numbers of mankind in an- " cient and modern times, &c." 8vo, Edinburgh, 1753. The author ſeems clearly to prove the point propoſed, (viz. " The ſuperior populouſneſs of antiquity.)" and having collected for that purpoſe a variety of examples, drawn from the ancient hiſtorians of ſeveral different nations, and delivered them with very judicious remarks and arguments of his own, his work, upon the whole, may be particularly uſeful in correcting the errors of ſome daring modern critics, who inconſiderately preſume to cavil at the *large numbers* mentioned in the Old Teſtament.

" happen

" happen to produce; yet it muſt be con- " feſſed, that conſidering it only with re- " ſpect to the phænomenon we are at pre- " ſent examining, it ſeems probable, that " the ancient condition of ſervants contri- " buted ſomething to the greater populouſ- " neſs of antiquity, and that the ancient " Slaves were more ſerviceable in raiſing up " people, than the inferior ranks of men in " modern times." But in his appendix, he ſpeaks of Slavery with leſs caution; ſo that his expreſſions are too liable to be made uſe of by the advocates for bondage, in favour of their pernicious doctrines; for he has inadvertently neglected to guard againſt any ſuch application, though the ſame would certainly be very diſagreeable to a perſon of his benevolent principles.

He obſerves in a note, (p. 208.) that " as " the ancient Slavery contributed to the " populouſneſs of the world, ſo it was " accompanied with *ſeveral other advan-* " *tages*, &c." And then he gives a long quotation from *Buſbequius*, wherein Slavery is repreſented in a much more agreeable dreſs than it deſerves. But this remark, that " the ancient Slavery contributed to " the populouſneſs of the world, &c." is no juſt argument in favour of Slavery in general,

general, neither have I any reaſon to ſuppoſe, that it was intended as ſuch by the worthy author. It proves only, that the advantages of the ancient Slavery were increaſed in proportion as the ſame approached nearer to *a well regulated liberty*, and was more diſtant from abſolute bondage; and therefore thoſe advantages ought rather to be attributed to the "*equitable* "*laws*" and cuſtoms, which *reſtrained* the behaviour of the ancient maſters, and *diminiſhed the bondage* of their ſervants, than to a general toleration of Slavery.

This may be demonſtrated by a quotation from the former part of the ſame work, p. 90. where the author, ſpeaking of the *antient Slaves*, informs us, that— "In ſome ſtates, particularly at Athens, "*equitable laws* were enacted for their ſe- "curity; they were treated with gentleneſs "and mildneſs, and allowed to acquire "riches, on paying a ſmall yearly tribute "to their maſters; nay, if they could "ſcrape together as much as could pur- "chaſe their liberty, their maſters were "obliged to ſet them free. Upon the "whole, they ſeem to have been more "certain of ſubſiſtence, and to have been

"better

" better fed, not only than the beggars, " but even many of the day labourers, and " lower order of the farmers and tradeſ- " men of modern times. It would be " chiefly where Slaves were treated with " equity and mildneſs, lived in friendſhip " with their maſters, were looked on as " part of the family, and intereſted in its " welfare, that this inſtitution could beſt " ſerve to render nations populous: on the " other hand, if they were cruelly uſed, " and their ſpirits broken with ſevere bon- " dage, they muſt have been leſs fit either " for labour or propagation."—That this latter is certainly the caſe in the Engliſh plantations, is proved (I hope) in the courſe of my work, and therefore the queries offered by the abovementioned author in his Appendix, (p. 207 and 208.) referring us "*to* " *the Maxims of our Planters*," in favour of propagation, will afford us no proof that the modern Weſt Indian Slavery is not deſtructive of the human ſpecies, howſoever ſenſible the planters may be, that it is their intereſt to remedy the evil, and "*en-* " *courage the breed* of Slaves as much as " they can." For it is plain, that (though they call themſelves Chriſtians, yet) they

 want

want thoſe "*equitable laws*," and humane regulations of the *ancient heathens*, to lighten the bondage of their Slaves, ſo that propagation and increaſe, muſt be greatly hindered. This objection does not in the leaſt affect the general point of the ſaid author's examination. He ſufficiently proves the lenity of the ancient maſters, and conſequently accounts for the great increaſe of their Slaves.

If the propagation of Slaves in the Engliſh plantations bears no proportion thereto, the extreme ſeverity of modern Slavery in many reſpects (of which I have given ample proofs) is the apparent obſtacle. The ſame author allows, indeed, in p. 207. that " modern Slavery ſeems to be on a " much worſe footing than the ancient. " In particular, (ſays he) Slavery in Tur- " key, Algiers, Tunis, Tripoli, Morocco, " and other African countries, is both very " ſevere, and under bad regulations:" but I am inclined to think, that it cannot poſſibly in any place be more ſevere, than it is even in our own colonies. Sorry am I, that ſuch unqueſtionable proofs of this, are ſo eaſily produced, even from the very laws

of

of our plantations, which ought rather to be calculated to prevent ſuch abuſes!

But the moſt "*equitable law,*" cannot render the admiſſion of Slavery either ſafe to this community, or juſtifiable in itſelf, becauſe the leaſt toleration of Slavery, or the allowing of *private property in the perſon of men,* will be liable in time, to introduce ſuch a *general bondage of the common people* *, as muſt inevitably affect the ſafety of regal government, by once more ſtrengthening the power of rich and overgrown ſubjects, with another dangerous vaſſalage, which will not eaſily be ſhaken off, if it ſhould once more take place; witneſs the oppoſition of John of Gaunt, and others of the nobility, in the reign of Richard II. † when the govern-

* Witneſs the oppreſſion which has been introduced even into our own colonies, Virginia, Barbadoes, &c. whereby thoſe that are called *free* Negroes, Mulattos, and Indians, as well as white ſervants and labourers, are rendered much more abject than the ancient Slaves. See notes in pages 49—75.

† "The minor King had been adviſed, by one part "of his council, to *increaſe* the power of the *lower people,* "and to leſſen that of the barons; in conſequence of "this a proclamation iſſued, which, amongſt other "things, directed, "Quod nulla acra terræ quæ in "*bondagio* vel *ſervitio* tenetur, altiùs quàm ad quatuor "denarios haberetur; & ſi qua ad minùs antea tenta "fuiſſet, in poſterùm non exaltaretur." John of Gaunt

 "put

ment thought it expedient for the maintenance of royal authority, to relieve the common people from bondage. " Nor is " the ſafety of a prince ſo firm and well " eſtabliſhed upon any other bottom, as " the general *ſafety*, and thereby *ſatisfaction of the common people*, which make " the bulk and ſtrength of all great kingdoms, whenever they conſpire and unite " in any common paſſion or intereſt. For " the nobles, without them, are but like " an army of officers without ſoldiers, and " make only a vain ſhew or weak noiſe, " unleſs raiſed and encreaſed by the voice " of the people, which, for this reaſon, is, in " a common Latin proverb, called *the* " *Voice of God*." (See Sir William Temple's Introduction to the Hiſtory of England, 3d edition, London 1708.)

" put himſelf at the head of the barons faction, and " procured a proclamation, repealing the former, in the " year following." (See the Hon. Mr. Juſtice Barrington's Obſervations on the more ancient Statutes, &c. 3d edit. p. 271. for which he quotes Rymer, vol. iii. p. 124.) The ſame author alſo quotes (from Brady, vol. iii. p. 393.) a further inſtance of the dangerous and ſelfiſh tyranny of the barons.—" In the fifteenth " year of this King, (ſays he) the barons petitioned " the King, *that no villeyn ſhould ſend his ſon to ſchool*; to " which the King gave the proper anſwer of *s'aviſera*."

On

On the other hand, if we were for a moment to ſuppoſe, that civil Slavery is in itſelf profitable and convenient for the community in general, and that the laborious part of mankind ought therefore to be held in bondage; I ſay, if we could ſuppoſe, that this were really true, we muſt neceſſarily condemn thoſe juſt encomiums which the author of the Diſſertations on the Numbers of Mankind, has beſtowed on the Britiſh government, (ſee p. 155 and 156 *) for having procured the reduction of vaſſalage in Scotland. But as no reaſonable perſon will deny, that the ſaid pru-

* "The late unprovoked rebellion, raiſed by the "rude inhabitants of theſe wilds, in order to dethrone "the beſt of Kings, to overturn the beſt of govern- "ments, and to undo the liberty of Britain, having "come to ſo great and ſo unexpected an height, and "having thereby awakened the attention of the govern- "ment, as well as that of others, who had influence "with thoſe in the adminiſtration of affairs, has pro- "duced ſome excellent laws, by which the liberty of "the whole country is better ſecured, manufactures, "and other kinds of labour are encouraged and pro- "moted in *Scotland*, and the inhabitants of the High- "lands may be brought from a ſtate of barbarity and "ſlavery, to a ſtate of civility and independence. By "the happy influence of theſe laws, a ſpirit for in- "duſtry has ſeized the minds of the people, and in a "few years wrought no inconſiderable change on the "country. Indeed it is impoſſible to expreſs, how "great obligations every loyal ſubject to his Majeſty, "every zealous friend to the Proteſtant ſucceſſion,

"and

dent and ſalutary meaſure is worthy of all the encomiums of this learned author, we cannot by any means admit the contrary maxim of *Buſbequius*, which is included in the long quotation made from him by the ſame author in his Appendix, p. 209, viz. " *Scio* " *ſervitii varia eſſe incommoda, ſed ea com-* " *modorum pondere ſublevantur.*"

Howſoever reaſonable this doctrine might appear to the miniſter of a German Emperor, (who moreover was reconciled, by long reſidence in an enſlaved country, to the arbitrary government of another Emperor ſtill more deſpotic than his own maſter) yet ſurely with Engliſhmen, it ought to be held in abhorrence. And indeed the worthy author who made the quotation, (though he thereby ſeems to honour it with his aſſent) has nevertheleſs furniſhed me, in another place, with ſuch very ſenſible arguments againſt it, that I am perſuaded no after conſiderations what-

" and every ſincere aſſerter of the liberty of Britain, " has to thoſe, whoſe hearty regard to the intereſt of " their country, has produced the happy proſpect we " have at preſent, of living for the future in peace, " and ſeeing liberty penetrate into the moſt remote " parts of the iſland."

ſoever, (even though they ſhould be expreſſed in the moſt maſterly manner by the ſame able author himſelf) can poſſibly invalidate them. "After all (ſays he) it is "not eaſy, if it be not altogether impoſ-"ſible, for a man of humanity to recon-"cile himſelf perfectly to the inſtitution "of domeſtic Slavery. With whatever "particular advantages it may be accom-"panied, one can ſcarce ever think of it "without ſenſible horror and deep com-"paſſion. Like too many of the barba-"rous and inhuman cuſtoms of the world, "it is highly diſgraceful to human na-"ture: nor can it ever produce *any ad-"vantages, which might not be gained by a "better and more human policy*." (P. 90, 91.)

All laws ought to be founded upon the principle of "*doing as one would be done "by*:" and indeed this principle ſeems to be the very baſis of the Engliſh conſtitution; for what precaution could poſſibly be more effectual for that purpoſe, than the right which we enjoy of being *judged by our peers*, creditable perſons of the vicinage; eſpecially, as we may likewiſe claim the right of excepting againſt any particular juryman, who might be ſuſpected of partiality?

 This

This law breathes the pure ſpirit of liberty, equity and ſocial love; being calculated to maintain that conſideration and mutual regard, which one perſon ought to have for another, howſoever unequal in rank or ſtation.

But when any part of the community, under the pretence of *private property*, is deprived of this common privilege, 'tis a violation of civil liberty, which is entirely inconſiſtent with the ſocial principles of a free ſtate.

True liberty protects the labourer as well as his lord; preſerves the dignity of human nature, and ſeldom fails to render a province rich and populous: whereas on the other hand, a toleration of Slavery is the higheſt breach of ſocial virtue, and not only tends to depopulation, but too often renders the minds of both maſters and Slaves utterly depraved and inhuman, by the hateful extremes of exaltation and depreſſion.

If ſuch a toleration ſhould ever be generally admitted in England, (which God forbid!) we ſhall no longer deſerve to be eſteemed a *civilized* people: becauſe, when the cuſtoms of *uncivilized* nations, and the

uncivi-

uncivilized cuſtoms which diſgrace our own colonies are become ſo familiar, as to be permitted among us with impunity, we ourſelves muſt inſenſibly degenerate to the ſame degree of baſeneſs, with thoſe from whom ſuch bad cuſtoms were derived, and may too ſoon have the mortification to ſee the *hateful extremes of tyranny and Slavery foſtered under every roof.*

Then muſt the happy medium of *a well regulated liberty* be neceſſarily compelled to find ſhelter in ſome *more civilized* country, where ſocial virtue, and that divine precept, " *thou ſhalt love thy neighbour as thy-* " *ſelf,*" are better underſtood.

An attempt to prove the dangerous tendency, injuſtice and diſgrace of tolerating Slavery amongſt Engliſhmen, would in any former age have been eſteemed as ſuperfluous and ridiculous, as if a man ſhould undertake in a formal manner, to prove that *darkneſs* is not *light.*

Sorry am I, that the depravity of the preſent age has made a demonſtration of this kind neceſſary!

Now that I may ſum up the amount of what has been ſaid in a ſingle ſentence, I ſhall beg leave to conclude in the words of the great Sir Edward Coke, which, though ſpoken on a different occaſion, are yet applicable to this. See Ruſhworth's Hiſt. Collect. Ann. 1628. 4 Caroli, fol. 540.

" It would be no honour to a King or " kingdom, to be a King of Bondmen or " Slaves, the end of this would be both " *Dedecus* and *Damnum*, both to King and " kingdom, that in former times have " been ſo renowned."

END OF THE THIRD PART.

PART

PART IV.

Some remarks on the ancient Villenage, ſhewing, that the obſolete laws and cuſtoms, which favoured that horrid oppreſſion, cannot juſtify the admiſſion of the modern Weſt-India Slavery into this kingdom, nor the leaſt claim of property, or right of ſervice, deducible therefrom.

SINCE the foregoing three parts of this work have been communicated in MS. to my friends, I have frequently had the mortification to hear very ſenſible and learned perſons refer to the old villenage doctrines, in their examination of the preſent queſtion, concerning property in Slaves; and from thence they have inſinuated a ſort of legal propriety in the pretenſions

tenſions of the modern Weſt-India Slave-holders, as if they could ſuppoſe, that a ſtate of Slavery might ſtill exiſt in this kingdom according to law.

This has happened not only in private converſation, but alſo lately in open court, and is therefore become a matter of very ſerious conſideration.

It is neceſſary, however, to be obſerved, that a retroſpect to ſuch obſolete cuſtoms, may very fairly be eſteemed a tacit acknowledgment, that neither the preſent laws in force, nor the preſent conſtitution and cuſtoms of England, can afford my opponents the leaſt juſtification for ſuch opinions, or they would not be obliged to go ſo far back for precedents.

But if ſuch obſolete doctrines are admitted as a rule in one caſe, (howſoever trivial) they certainly are liable to be admitted likewiſe in others of more importance, becauſe uſage * muſt neceſſarily revive them, and give them, once more, the force of laws: ſo that we ought to be extremely jealous of the leaſt tendency to ſuch a revival, as the ſame would be a very

* "*Uſage and Cuſtom* generally received, do *obtinere* "*vim legis*," &c. Hale's Hiſt. of Common Law, p. 65.

dangerous

dangerous enemy to the freedom of the common people in general.

The pernicious effects of reviving the doctrines of villenage, at firſt, perhaps, would be felt by none but the poor wretched Negroes themſelves, and therefore, the ſubſequent evils may (like objects at a diſtance) ſeem leſs, at firſt ſight, than they really are.

But let us take a nearer view of them—If the preſent Negroes are once permitted to be retained as Slaves in England, by enforcing the cuſtoms of villenage, their poſterity, though Engliſhmen born, will be condemned of courſe, by the ſame laws and cuſtoms, * to the perpetual tyranny of their maſters; and the mixed people or Mulattoes, produced by the unavoidable intercourſe with their white neighbours, will be alſo ſubject to the like bondage with their unhappy parents.

* "The writ *de nativo habendo* lieth for the lord, who "claimeth the inheritance in any villain, when his vil-"lain is run from him, &c." Natura Brevium, p. 171. ——So that the poor Slave, it is plain, could not avail himſelf of the Engliſhmen's *Birth- right*, though a natural born ſubject; for his being a NATIVE, did rather *confirm his bondage* (according to the unjuſt laws and cuſtoms of villenage) than entitle him to freedom.

Thus

Thus it is obvious, that a foundation would be laid for a moſt dangerous vaſſalage, in which the poorer ſort, even of the original Engliſh themſelves, might in time be involved, through their inability to oppoſe the unjuſt claims, which ſome haughty land-holders might once more think fit to aſſume—For as it is much eaſier to do wrong, than to obtain right or juſtice, ſo it would be much eaſier for a rich land-holder to aſſume the lord paramount, and detain a poor perſon born upon his eſtate, under the pretence of being his *native* or villain by preſcription, than for ſuch an injured perſon to maintain his cauſe, without money or friends, againſt his powerful oppreſſor.

It will therefore be expedient to examine how far ſuch obſolete doctrines may, or may not be admitted as a rule in the preſent diſpute.

The doctrines and cuſtoms relating to villenage are of two kinds, 1ſt, ſome enforce that horrid tyranny; 2dly, others reſtrain it.

The firſt kind were originally introduced by an unjuſt *uſurpation* * (" quia, ab homi-

* " Quia conſuetudo, contra rationem introducta, " potius *uſurpatio* quam conſuetudo appellari debet." 2 Inſt.

" ne, et pro vicio introducta est servitus, " &c." Fortescue.) and in themselves are contrary to *the law of nature, reason, and common equity.*——" For, CRUEL of ne- " cessity must that law be counted, which " augmenteth Slavery and diminisheth " freedom." &c. *

But the second division of villenage doctrines and customs are of a very different nature, being in favour of liberty: they seem to have arisen chiefly from the charitable efforts of the ancient lawyers, to re-

2 Inst. ch. x. sect. clxix.—" Fuerunt etiam in con- " questu liberi homines, qui liberè tenuerunt tene- " menta sua per libera servitia, vel per liberas consuetu- " dines, et cum per potentiores ejecti essent; post mo- " dum reversi receperunt eadem tenementa sua tenen- " da in villenagio." &c. Hen. de Bracton, de legibus et consuetudinibus Angliæ, ch. xi. p. 7.

And a Villain Regardent was made a Villain in Gross, (not for any fault in himself, or with his own consent but) merely by the *arbitrary act* of his lord, *in* granting him by his deed to another, " *par son fait*" (says Littleton) " a une autre donqs il est Villein en Grosse et nemy regardant." 2 Inst. ch. ii. sect. clxxxi.

* CRUDELIS etiam necessario judicabitur lex, quæ servitutem augmentat, & minuit libertatem. Nam *pro ea natura semper implorat humana.* Quia, ab homine, et pro vicio, introducta est servitus. Sed libertas a Deo hominis est indita naturæ. Quare ipsa ab homine sublata semper redire gliscit, ut facit omne, quod libertate naturali privatur. Quò IMPIUS et CRUDELIS *judicandus est qui libertati non favet.* Hæc considerantia Angliæ jura in omni casu *libertati dant favorem.* (Chan. Fort. de laudibus legum, ch. xlii. p. 101.)

strain

ſtrain and reduce villenage; and certainly may ſtill be effectual for the like benevolent purpoſe in all ſimilar caſes, becauſe they are not repugnant to the ſound principles of the common law; whereas the doctrines under the firſt head, are plainly contrary to reaſon and nature, and therefore muſt neceſſarily be conſidered as null and void——Quia in conſuetudinibus non diuturnitas temporis, ſed ſoliditas rationis eſt conſideranda, (2 Inſt. p. 141. note.)

Even ſo early as the Saxon times, an attempt was made to reſtrain theſe diſgraceful and uncivilized cuſtoms of our anceſtors; for the Confeſſor's laws ordained, " that the lords ſhould ſo demean them-" ſelves towards their men, that they " neither incur GUILT AGAINST GOD, " nor OFFENCE againſt the KING; or " which is all one" (ſays my author) " to " reſpect them as GOD's PEOPLE, and the " KING's SUBJECTS." (Bacon's Government of England, part i. ch. xix. p. 57.)

This religious and juſt ſpirit of the Confeſſor's laws ſeemed to be retained by our ancient lawyers, even after the conqueſt, when the Feudal tyranny was at the greateſt height.

They

They took all favourable opportunities to enfranchiſe * the villain——If the lord was negligent in purſuing or claiming the fugitive villein for a year, they granted to the villein a privilege afterwards of returning and defending himſelf in a free ſtate, when it was "*not* LAWFUL *nor* " SAFE *for the lord to retake him.*——" non erit domino LICITUM *nec* TUTUM manum apponere †, &c.

* " En pluſurs maneres purra home recoverer fraunk- " eſtaté, &c. Britton, 2d edit. p. 78.
—" ſi come par brefe de Mordaunceſtæ, et par reys " ſe abaterent les brefs iſſint, que il ad demurré en nos " demeynes terres ou aillours en aſcune de nos villes " ou de nos cytes par un an et un jour ſaunz chalenge " le pleyntyfe, et demaunde jugement ſi il deyve en tiel " cas reſpondre et cele excepcion puſſe avoire; en tiel " cas ſoit le ſeigniour forjuge de accion pur ſa negli- " gence, et auſi ou le demaundaunt purra averrer par " record de notre court, que ſon ſeigniour le ad ſuffert " aſcient en jures, et en enqueſtes en noſtre court come " fraunk home, et auſi ſi il puſſe averrer par record que " il eyt recovere fraunk tenement de luy par jugement " de noſtre court, ou le pleyntyſe ne allegga nul ex- " cepcion encontre luy de naifté, &c." Britton, p. 83.

† " Si autem Dominus ille negligens fuerit in proſe- " quendo, et in clameo apponendo qualitercunque; ſi " fugitivus revertatur poſt annum, non erit domino " *licitum* nec *tutum* manum apponere, tamen poſt an- " num poteſt fugitivus habere privilegium, et ſe in " ſtatu libero defendere per exceptionem, et ſic ſolvitur " dominica poteſtas. Et dicuntur ſervi eſſe in ſtatu " libero, donec dominus verſus eos ſibi perquiſerit per " legem terræ, nec habebit poteſtatem aliquam in eis " vel liberis ſuis, terris vel aliis bonis ipſorum, donec " corpus, quod principale eſt, diſrationaverit, ſecun-

When the lord loſt poſſeſſion of the fugitive villein through *negligence*, or even through *inability to detain him* (per *negligentiam* vel *impotentiam**) he might not afterwards take him; ſo that force was as good a title, it ſeems, for the commencement of the *Villein's liberty*, as it had before been for the commencement of *the lord's property*; and was preferred in law.

The King's courts, in thoſe ancient times, were ſo manifeſtly diſpoſed to favour liberty, that it ſeemed to be their endeavour to render the lord's ſuit *de nativo habendo*, as difficult † and precarious as poſſi-

" dum quod inferiùs dicetur." Hen. de Bracton de Legibus et Conſuetudinibus Angliæ, cap. x. p. 7. folio edit. 1569.

* " Cûm autem Dominus per negligentiam *vel impotentiam* ſui ſeyſinam de ſuo fugitivo amiſerit, ſi reſumptis viribus contra privilegium, fugitivum reduxerit, vel cum fugitivus redierit, ipſum retinuerit, *poenam debitam non evadet*, cûm hoc ſit contra pacem. —Sed ſi extra villenagium, S. perlapſum 3 vel 4 dierum inventus fuerit cûm dominus negligens fuerit in proſequutione, capi non poterit nec detineri, nec magis quam liber homo, et ſi fuerit, inde habebit *querelam de impriſonamento*." Ibid.

† " If the villain ſay, that he is a freeman, &c. then the ſheriff *ought not to ſeize him*, but then the lord ought to ſue a *Pone* to remove the plea before the juſtices in the Common Pleas, or before the juſtices in eyre.—But if the villain purchaſe a writ *de libertate probanda*, before the lord hath ſued the *Pone* to remove the plea before the juſtices, then that writ of *libertate probanda* is a ſuperſedeas unto the lord, that " he

ble; when, at the ſame, the Villein's ſuit *de libertate probanda* * was indulged with as many advantages † as the lawyers could well venture to give it, conſidering the ſeverity of the times in which they lived.

Nay, their humanity and juſtice even outwent the temper of thoſe rude times;

"he proceed not upon the writ of *nativo habendo* till "the eyre of the juſtices, or till the day the plea be "adjourned before the juſtices, and that the lord *ought* "*not to ſeize the villain* in the mean time." See Sir Anthony Fitzherbert's Natura Brevium, firſt publiſhed in the reign of King Henry VIII. (6th edit. p. 171.)

* "Ceo brefe de peas eſt appelé brefe de fraunchiſe "en favour de fraunchiſe, et eſt plus toſt pledable, que "neſt brefe de naifté, &c." Britton, p. 80.

† "—It appeareth in 12 Henry III. Itin. North, "that the villain ſued a *libertate probanda* et obtulet ſe, "at the fourth day againſt the lord, and he did not "appear, but made default, for which, upon the de- "fault of the lord, *the villain was enfranchiſed*; and he "had a writ unto the ſheriff, *that he do not ſuffer the lord* "*to trouble him after*. (Natura Brevium, p. 173.)—And "a man can join in a writ of *nativo habendo*, *but two* "*villains*, BUT IN FAVOUR OF LIBERTY, *many villains* "*may join in a libertate probanda*. (Id. 174.)

"If two bring a *nativo habendo*, the nonſuit of one "of them, is the nonſuit of them both; for ſummons "and ſeverance lieth not in that writ. But in a *liber-* "*tate probanda*, it is otherwiſe, for there the nonſuit "of the one *ſhall not prejudice the other*." (Id. 175.)

"——Et le plaintiffe dit que il eſt franke, &c.—And "the plaintiff (being a villain) ſaith, that he is free, "and of a free eſtate, and not a villain, this ſhall be "tried in the county where the plaintiff hath conceived "his action, and *not in the county where the manor is*, and "this is (IN FAVOREM LIBERTATIS) in favour of "liberty." Littleton, lib. ii. cap. xi. ſect. 193. p. 124 b.

 and,

and, as too great forwardneſs in the cauſe of *liberty* is apt to confirm, rather than weaken the contrary extreme of *tyranny*, ſo it happened with reſpect to Villenage; for the apparent partiality of the courts in favour of the Villein, did (undeſignedly on their part) occaſion a confirmation by Statute law, of that unjuſt uſurpation, which required a more moderate and gradual oppoſition to reduce it.

The puiſſance of the Barons was then too great to be effectually controuled by the equity of the *common law*; and the legiſlature (in which the landed intereſt in thoſe early times was much too predominant) ſeemed to be offended with the manifeſt inclination of the profeſſors of the common law (the judges and lawyers) to favour liberty, and impede the ſuits of the lord.— Juſtice, therefore, muſt give place to the private intereſt of ſuch powerful land-holders, and the lord's prerogative muſt be inſured to him by act of parliament.

Two acts * were accordingly paſſed in two different reigns, which expreſly reſtrained the uſe of writs *de libertate probanda*.

Yet theſe obſtacles ſerved only to render the humanity and perſeverance of our an-

* 25 Edward III. c. xviii. and 9 Richard II. c. ii.

cient

cient patriotic lawyers more conſpicuous, and their ſucceſs more meritorious; for the interpretation of the law ſtill continued *in favour of liberty*, ſo that the maxim of chancellor Forteſcue, in the 47th chapter of his book, de Laudibus Legum Angliæ, ſeems to have been grounded on the practice of his predeceſſors.——" humana natura, in *libertatis* cauſa, *favorem ſemper* " magis quam in cauſis aliis deprecetur." And in the 42d chapter, p. 101, he ſays, " Angliæ Jura in omni caſu *libertati* dant " favorem."

Nevertheleſs, the bondage of Villenage remained even in his time; and though he condemned *as cruel*, thoſe laws, which augmented Slavery, yet, where the free conſent of the parties might be implied,—his objections were removed.—Upon this footing he excuſed the law which made the free-woman bond, when ſhe ſubmitted herſelf in marriage to a bondman, becauſe, ſaid he, " of her own free-will * ſhe hath " made herſelf a bond-woman, not forced " thereto by the law; much like to ſuch

* ——" Proprio arbitrio ſe fecit ancillam, ſed potius " ſervam, nullatenus a lege coacta, qualiter et faciunt " qui ſe ſervos reddunt in curiis regum, vel in ſervi- " tutem ſe vendunt, nullatenus ad hoc compulſi." Forteſcue, cap. 42. p. 102.

" as in King's courts become bond-men, " or ſell themſelves into bondage without " any compulſion * at all.

But even this doctrine, which Sir John Forteſcue was willing to excuſe, was thought too ſevere † by his ſucceſſors in the law; who, inſtead of neglecting the old cuſtoms which favoured the Villein, ventured even to add others to them for the ſame beneficent purpoſe.

Every negligence or delay of the lord in proſecuting his claim, was interpreted to the advantage of the Villein, in the King's courts, which were always open to his complaints; and if the lord attempted to put an end to the Villein's ſuit, by forcibly eſloining his body, the plaintiff (or the ſheriff, in his behalf) was allowed a "*Capias in* "*Withernam*, ‡ to take the defendant's

* This is ſimilar to the practice allowed by the 13th ſection of the Habeas Corpus act.

† ——" And that IN FAVOUR OF LIBERTY; for a " free woman ſhall not be a villain for taking of a " villain to be her huſband." Fitzherbert's Natura Brevium, p. 174.

‡ The uſe of this writ, (as explained by the late learned Judge Forteſcue Aland) is "*to take his body*" (the body of the plagiary) "*by way of repriſal.*"—— This is certainly very reaſonable and juſt; though, I am perſuaded, ſuch doctrine will not be reliſhed by our modern Weſt India Slaveholders, who, in defiance of our laws, do frequently preſume to kidnap and forcibly tranſport their quondam Slaves.——However, as they ought

" body, and to keep the ſame, quouſque, " &c. whether he be *a peer of this realm*, or " other perſon." (See judge Fitzherbert's Natura Brevium, p. 151. vi. edit.)—Again, a Villein was enfranchiſed " *by the cuſtom of* " *London*, if he dwelt for a year and a day within the city." (ſee lord chief baron Comyns his digeſt of the laws of England.)

Another remarkable obſervation is likewiſe made by the ſame author in favour of the Villein, for, ſays he, " in an action " for the trial of his liberty, as *libertate* " *probanda, homine replegiando*, &c. IT IS " NO PLEA that the plaintiff is his Vil- " lein."

At length, by the repeated diſcouragements which Villenage met with in the Courts of law, and perhaps in ſome meaſure likewiſe, by the more civilized and chriſtian diſpoſition of the lords * them-

ought not to be ignorant of this doctrine, it is certainly better, that they ſhould be taught by friendly information, than rude experience.

* ——" But the ſervant's merit, and the lord's be- " nignity concurring with ſome conſcience of religion, " as the light grew more clear, abated the rigour of the " tenure into that which we now call copyhold." (Bacon's Government of England, part I. chap. xxxi. p. 75.)

——" Further, the ſame peaceable manners made the " minds of men be ſhock'd with the bondage of their " follow-creatures; villains were enfranchiſed, the ſla-

ſelves, this deteſtable practice of holding men in an involuntary ſtate of bondage became entirely out of uſe in this kingdom, inſomuch, that a ſingle *Villein*, according to the old acceptation of the word, (I wiſh I might ſay ſo of the preſent) has not been known for many ages; * unleſs the copy-holders may be ſo called: but their condition is at preſent ſo much more honourable than Villenage, that it cannot juſtly be compared with it.

"The tenant" (ſays Mr. Sheppard, ſpeaking of copy-holders) " was anciently " a bondman, and his tenure a baſe tenure: " *but time hath changed both*, and now, he " and his eſtate both are ſo far free, that " if he pay his rents, and do his ſervices

" viſh tenure of villenage, which had taken its name " from the objects of it, was deemed to be too ſevere, " and by degrees was converted into ſoccage, a tenure " better accommodated to the more civilized diſpoſi- " tions of mankind.——Thus the tenure by knight's " ſervice, and the tenure by villenage, the one ſinking, " and the other riſing in dignity, falling both gradu- " ally into the balance of ſoccage tenure, this laſt ex- " tended itſelf daily in Great Britain over land pro- " perty." (Dalrymple's Hiſtory of Feudal Property, p. 26.)

* " For Sir Thomas Smith (Commonwealth, b. iii. " c. x.) teſtifies, that in all his time, (and he was ſecre- " tary to Edward VI.) he never knew any villein in " groſs throughout the realm, &c." (Blackſtone's Comment. b. ii. p. 96. 3d edit.)

according

" according to the cuſtom of the place, " the lord cannot hurt him or his eſtate." (Court-keeper's Guide, p. 96.)

From what has been ſaid I hope it will plainly appear, that Villenage no longer ſubſiſts in this kingdom; that the doctrines (under the firſt head) which formerly enforced it, are now entirely obſolete; and that the doctrines and cuſtoms under the ſecond head, were the means whereby they became ſo. " Quia conſuetudo *ex* CERTA " CAUSA RATIONABILI *uſitata* privat com- " munem legem." (Littleton, lib. ii. ch. x. ſect. clxix.)

The reaſonable cauſe for the uſe of the latter, is frequently expreſſed in the foregoing quotations of them, " ET CEO EST IN " FAVOREM LIBERTATIS." (Littleton, p. 124.) or to that effect.——So *that* THE FAVOURING OF LIBERTY ſeemed to be an eſtabliſhed maxim with the ancient lawyers, to whom indeed we are principally indebted for this ſignal improvement of our conſtitution.

What then can excuſe the very different behaviour of our modern lawyers * in at-

* Leſt this cenſure ſhould ſeem too general, it may, perhaps, be neceſſary to obſerve, that there are ſtill *ſome* gentlemen of the law, who (to the author's own know-

tempting to revive the oppreſſive doctrines of Villenage, which their honeſt predeceſſors always laboured to aboliſh? Preſcription and cuſtom cannot now be pleaded, becauſe two incidents are wanting, which, in Lilly's abridgment, are ſaid to be *inſeparable from cuſtom*, viz. 1ſt, "*A* "*reaſonable commencement*," (for "all cuſ-"toms and preſcriptions that be againſt "reaſon, are void." 2 Inſt. p. 140.) 2dly, "*Continuance without interruption*;" which is alſo manifeſtly wanting, becauſe no ſuch Slaviſh cuſtoms have ſubſiſted within the memory of man; or I may add, for many generations of men; ſo that *preſcription*

knowledge) are as thoroughly ſenſible of the injuſtice and impropriety of tolerating Slavery in this kingdom, as their predeceſſors. There muſt undoubtedly be a great many others likewiſe of the ſame opinion, though unknown to the author. Nevertheleſs thoſe gentlemen of the law, whoſe contrary doctrines I am unfortunately obliged to oppoſe, are numerous, eminent and learned; and ſome of them (with reſpect to the proceedings of a late trial) have ſo far prevailed, as to give me very juſt reaſon to dread a confirmation by judicial authority of thoſe doctrines againſt which I contend. Therefore it is incumbent on every lawyer who is a well-wiſher to the civil liberties of mankind, to take the firſt opportunity of diſclaiming, and publickly proteſting againſt all doctrines which may tend to the introduction of the Weſt India Slavery, *or the leaſt right or property* in the involuntary ſervice of our fellow-ſubjects, ariſing from the ſame, otherwiſe the odium muſt neceſſarily fall upon the whole body in general.

and

and cuſtom, which originally were the chief pillars and ſupport of all claims under Villenage, are now *abſolutely againſt it* ; for, " as USAGE is a good interpreter of laws, " ſo NON-USAGE *where there is no example,* " *is a great intendment that the law will not* " *bear it,*" &c. (2d. Inſt. ch. iv. p. 81. b. notes.)

Sir Matthew Hale, (lord chief juſtice) in his Analyſis of the law, obſerves, on the title of Lord and Villein, that " it is at this " day of little uſe, *and in effect is altogether* " *antiquated.*" * (ſect. xxi. p. 50.)—But with whatſoever propriety, cuſtoms, and alſo ſome particular doctrines of the common law, may be ſaid to become obſolete and antiquated, yet the ſame could not rightly be ſaid of the *ſtatute law*, (I ſpeak, with reference to the two Acts of Parliament † which formerly enforced the lord's claim on his Villein) unleſs ſome very material alteration concerning this point, had ſince been made therein *by the ſame authority* ; ‡ becauſe, " an Act of Parliament by *non*

* See the ſame author, p. 4. " Villeins," (ſays he) " now antiquated."

† 25 Edward III. c. xviii. and 9 Richard II. c. ii.

‡ (By the ſame authority.) " Unumquodque diſſolvi-" tur *eo modo quo colligatur.*" Noy's Maxims, p. 4.

" *uſer*

" *uſer* can(not) be antiquated or loſe its " force." (ſee 2 Inſt. p. 81 b. note.)

Neverthelefs, the advocates for Slavery cannot avail themſelves of theſe ſtatutes; becauſe *Villenage* (being originally a tenure of land,) " was taken away and diſcharged" by authority of parliament in the 12 year of Charles II. *—So that the ſaid ſtatutes are rendered uſeleſs by this ſubſequent act. —*Villenage*, indeed, is not nominally aboliſhed by this act; yet, as *all tenures* were thereby reduced " *to free and common ſoc-* " *cage*," † it is neceſſarily implied, that this baſe and moſt diſgraceful branch of

* Cap. xxiv. " An act for taking away the court of " wards and liveries, and tenures in capite, and by " knight's ſervice and purveyance, and for ſettling a " revenue upon his Majeſty in lieu thereof."

" Whereas it hath been found by *former experience*, " that the courts of wards and liveries, and tenures by " knight's ſervice, either of the King or others, or by " knight's ſervice in capite, or ſoccage in capite of the " King, AND THE CONSEQUENTS UPON THE SAME, " *have been much more burthenſome, grievous and prejudi-* " *cial to the kingdom, than they have been beneficial to the* " *King*, &c."

† " And all tenures of any honors, manors, lands, " tenements or hereditaments, or any eſtate of inheri- " tance at the common law, held either of the King, " *or of any other perſon or perſons, bodies politic or corpo-* " *rate*, are hereby enacted to be *turned into* FREE AND " COMMON SOCCAGE, *to all intents and purpoſes*, &c. " *any law, ſtatute, cuſtom, or uſage*, to the contrary " hereof in anywiſe notwithſtanding." Id.

the

the old feudal tenures, was lopped off at the ſame time with the reſt. *

Nevertheleſs, when I have urged the force of this act for the entire abolition of villenage, I have been anſwered, that formerly there were two different degrees of villenage, and that the loweſt of theſe could not be diſſolved by the ſaid act, becauſe it was not *a tenure of lands*, and therefore could not be ſaid, according to the terms of the act, to be reduced to "*free and common ſoccage*;" and that it was ſo far from the *condition of a tenure*, that all thoſe unhappy people called *villains in groſs*, were themſelves conſidered in law merely as the *perſonal* † *property* of their lords.

But let it be remembered nevertheleſs, (what I have before hinted) that ſuch barbarous cuſtoms had no other foundation,

* "And that all tenures by knight's ſervice, &c. *and* "*the* FRUITS AND CONSEQUENTS *thereof*, *happened*, or "which ſhall or may hereafter happen or ariſe there-"upon or thereby, *be taken away and diſcharged*; *any* "*law*, *ſtatute*, *&c. notwithſtanding*." Id.

† "In groſſe: is that which belongs *to the perſon of* "*the lord*, and belongeth *not to any manor*, *lands*, &c." 2 Inſt. ch. xi. ſect. clxxxi. p. 120 b. note.

"Et come aſcun ſerra nèe ſerfe il ſerra *purement le* "*chatel* ſon ſeigniour a doner et a vendre a ſa volounté, "&c." Britton, p. 78 b.

than

than the violent and unchriſtian uſurpation of the uncivilized barons in an age of darkneſs; and that religion and morality, reaſon and the law of nature *(the very foundation of our* ENGLISH COMMON LAW) were obliged to give place to the imaginary (tho' miſtaken) intereſt, and uncontrolable power of theſe over-grown landholders.

" Theſe tenures and obligations aroſe " moſt of them at a time, *when the inte-" reſt of the ſuperior in the fief was extremely " ſtrong*, and were therefore moſt of them " in their origin *extremely ſevere.*" (See Dalrymple's Hiſtory of Feudal Property, p. 74.)

So that although this loweſt degree of bondage was not really a tenure, yet it certainly may be eſteemed an *appendage*, or rather *an incident* " FRUIT OR CONSEQUENT" of the *military tenures*, when *the feudal ſeverity was at the height*; and therefore, as the ſaid tenures were gradually reduced, ſo in proportion was the bondage leſſened, until " whatever remained in either country " (England or Scotland) of military te-" nures, WITH THE VARIOUS INCIDENTS, " FRUITS, AND DEPENDENCES *attending " them, was laid for ever to reſt.*" (Dalrymple, p. 74, 75.) And the ſame judicious writer

writer is of opinion (ſee p. 75.) that "this "was done in England during the reign "of Charles II." For this he refers to the 12 Car. II. cap. 24. Nevertheleſs a more reſtrained conſtruction has been put upon this act by the honourable Mr. Juſtice Barrington, in page 272, of his Obſervations on the ancient ſtatutes (3d edition, London 1769, p. 272.); for I ſuppoſe he ſpeaks of this act when he informs us, that "*the ſtatute of Charles* II. *(or rather of* "*Cromwell,)*" as he is pleaſed to ſay, "*aboliſhes* THOSE TENURES ONLY, *which* "*were attended with wardſhips, &c.*" Probably he was led to this opinion by the 7th ſection, which provides, "that this act, or "any thing therein contained, ſhall not "take away, or be conſtrued to take away "tenures in frank almoigne, &c.—nor to "alter or change any tenure by *copy of* "*court roll, or any ſervices incident there-* "*unto,* nor to take away the honorary "ſervices of grand *ſerjeanty,* OTHER THAN "OF WARDSHIP, &c." Nevertheleſs *wardſhip,* and the other articles expreſly mentioned after it, are not the only prerogatives which were taken away by this act; for if it were really ſo, all the former part of the act would be abſolutely uſeleſs and unintelligible.

telligible. The principal deſign of the legiſlature at that time, ſeems to have been the reduction of *all tenures whatſoever*, (whether " attended with wardſhips," &c. or held by knight's ſervice, &c. or otherwiſe) " *to free and common ſoccage:*" and as this point is ſo very clearly expreſſed in the body of the act, it certainly never could be intended to marr and annul that effect by *any after clauſe* in the ſame act.

It is therefore neceſſary to conſtrue the meaning of the 5th, 6th, and 7th ſections, agreeable to the apparent deſign of what goes before: and if this be done, the *general* ſenſe before quoted from Mr. Dalrymple, will be ſufficiently juſtified.—The deſign of the act is *expreſly*, that " all te-" nures by knights ſervice of the King, or " of any other perſon, and by knights ſer-" vice in capite, and by ſoccage in capite of " the King, AND THE FRUITS and CONSE-" QUENTS THEREOF, happened, or which " ſhall or may hereafter happen or ariſe " thereupon, or thereby, *be taken away* " *and diſcharged*; any law, ſtatute, cuſ-" tom, or uſage to the contrary hereof in " any wiſe notwithſtanding; and ALL TE-" NURES of ANY *honors*, *manors*, *lands*, " *tenements or hereditaments*, OR ANY *eſtate*

 " *of*

" *of inheritance at the common law, held either* " *of the King, or of any other perſon or per-* " *ſons,*" &c. (this muſt certainly include ALL TENURES *whatſoever*, whether " *attended* " *with wardſhips,*" &c. or otherwiſe) " are " hereby enacted to be TURNED INTO " FREE AND COMMON SOCCAGE, *to all in-* " *tents and purpoſes,*" &c. " *any law, ſta-* " *tute, cuſtom, or uſage,* to the contrary " hereof in any wiſe notwithſtanding."

Now, as Villenage was certainly one of " *the fruits* or CONSEQUENTS" of the arbitrary military tenures, it muſt inevitably have been annihilated by this reduction of the ſaid tenures, had it not been *extinct in itſelf*, for *want of ſucceſſion*, long before the making of the ſaid law; not a ſingle Villein (properly ſo called) having been known for ſeveral ages, as is before remarked. The *Extinction* of Villenage, therefore, (though not *effected* by this act, yet) was certainly *confirmed* by the ſaid act, and the revival of any ſuch old arbitrary claims is rendered abſolutely illegal thereby.

Neverthelefs, the honourable Mr. juſtice Barrington ſeems to be of a different opinion, in page 272; for though he there ſpeaks of Villenage as being " *entirely dropt* " *in this country,*"—yet he adds,—" *with-*

" *out its being aboliſhed by any ſtatute.*" And he further explains his meaning by the note before quoted, viz. that " *the ſtatute* " *of Charles II (or rather of Cromwell) abo-* " *liſhes* THOSE TENURES ONLY" (ſays he) " *which were attended with wardſhips,*" &c. But the words before quoted from the act, prove beyond diſpute, that ALL TENURES of ANY honors, manors, lands, &c. are thereby reduced to " FREE AND " COMMON SOCCAGE;" and conſequently the rights which are preſerved to the lords or owners of manors, &c. by the 5th, 6th, and 7th ſections, can only be ſuch as are not inconſiſtent with " *free and common* " *ſoccage;*" for the 5th ſection expreſly ſays, that the act " ſhall not be conſtrued to take " away any rents certain, herriots or ſuits " of court, belonging or incident to any for- " mer tenure, now taken away or allowed " by virtue of this act, "or " OTHER SER- " VICES INCIDENT OR BELONGING TO " TENURE IN COMMON SOCCAGE, &c."

The unnatural and unjuſt prerogative of the lords of manors over their natives or Villeins, (" for the nativus," ſays Mr. juſtice Barrington, " became a Villeyn, by " being born in ſervitude, *within a parti-* " *cular*

" *cular manor or district,*") * must necessarily be considered therefore, as " taken " away and discharged," because the same was certainly one of the *Fruits and consequents* of the former military tenures; and, as such, is inconsistent with " *tenure in " common soccage:*" so that if we were even to suppose, that a succession of natives or Villains, are still remaining on any particular honor, manor, land, &c. yet the present lord or possessor thereof, would not be able to maintain or claim the least authority or power of retaining such persons as his Villeins, or natives of his manor, for the reasons before given; because such a claim would be absolutely illegal, according to the true meaning and unavoidable construction of this act. The servile tenure of Villenage, however, was universally in England, improved into the present honourable tenure of copyhold, before the making of this act, and it was therefore just, that all *reasonable* claims, which at that time were *customarily* due to the lords of manors, should be reserved: and this seems to be the true intention and purpose of the 5th, 6th, and 7th sections. By the

* Observation on the more Ancient Statues, p. 275.

laſt of theſe, indeed, it is provided, that this act ſhall not "alter or change any te-"nure by copy of court-roll, or *any ſer-" vices incident thereunto*, &c."

Yet it cannot be ſuppoſed, that the legiſlature intended hereby to reſerve "any "ſervices" inconſiſtent with "*tenure in "common ſoccage*;" becauſe this would inevitably deſtroy the meaning, and fruſtrate the apparent deſign of the whole act. We may, therefore, very juſtly conclude with the learned and judicious Mr. Blackſtone, that "*Villenage was virtually "aboliſhed*"* by this act, though "*copy-"holds were reſerved.*"

Villenage, therefore, being certainly *extinct* in law, as well as *in itſelf, for want of ſucceſſion*, (which is before remarked) it would be very impolitic, as well as unjuſt, to permit a foreign † inſtitution, like the

* "And theſe encroachments grew to be ſo univer-"ſal, that when *tenure in villenage was virtually aboliſhed "(though copyholds were reſerved) by the ſtatute of Charles* "II. there was hardly a pure villein left in the nation." Commentaries on the Laws of England, b. ii. p. 96. edit. 3.

† —"The common law is now ſo much improved "by the active wiſdom of our legiſlatures, through "a long ſucceſſion of ages; is ſo peculiarly adapted to "the temper of the nation; and ſo well fortified by its "utility and good ſenſe; that *no foreign ſyſtem* could

Weſt Indian Slavery, to revive or aſſume, like a lawful heir, the ancient rights of Villenage, when it is apparent, that ſuch a claimant has no juſt title to ſucceed.

The Weſt Indian Slavery ſprung from a very different ſource, and therefore hereditary right by deſcent is excluded, eſpecially as this modern bondage did not even commence, *until the former had been many years extinct*; for it is a maxim in law, that "*cuſtoms cannot extend to things newly* "*created.*" Wood's Inſt. p. 11.

The only excuſe which can be alledged for tolerating this iniquitous and diſgraceful bondage, *even in the Weſt Indies*, is a preſumed neceſſity, ariſing (as intereſted perſons tell us) from the exceſſive heat of the climates where our colonies are ſituated; but as the ſaid ſuppoſed neceſſity is *merely local*, *ſo ought to be the toleration of it likewiſe*, if we might allow, that any neceſſity * whatſoever can juſtify it. (See notes from p. 49 to 73, in the 3d part.)

" ever expect to invade it with ſucceſs. Should the " attempt be made to import any ſtrange laws, con- " trary to the fundamental maxims of our own, it " would always be repulſed with that indignation it ſo " juſtly deſerves." Dr. Bever's Diſcourſe on Juriſprudence and the Civil Law, p. 15, 16.

* " Whatever neceſſity may be pleaded for it, it is " greatly to be lamented, that there is any ſuch thing

 " as

The plantation laws and cuſtoms therefore, with reſpect to their ſource, temper and neceſſity, muſt certainly be eſteemed as different *and diſtant* from our own, as the *climate itſelf*; which, in truth, is *ſo many degrees*, that the leaſt right or title *to the inheritance of the old Engliſh Villenage cannot poſſibly be admitted.*

Nay, this ſtranger is ſo far from having any relationſhip, that it has not even the leaſt *ſimilarity* to Villenage, except what conſiſts in cruel oppreſſion, and apparent immorality; and theſe, I hope, are no inducements for reviving the former tyranny: on the contrary, it will certainly *be a ſtain of everlaſting infamy on the preſent lawyers, (as well as on the age in which they live,)* if they do not demonſtrate *the unlawfulneſs* of admitting the leaſt claim of property in the perſons of men by THIS VERY SIMILARITY. For as the former tyranny was *un-*

"as Slavery any where. As Moſes ſaid, *Would God, that all the Lord's people were prophets!* ſo I would "ſay, Would God, that all mankind were free, that "thoſe who are bond were free, and that thoſe who "are free may ſo uſe their liberty, as not to abuſe it "unto licentiouſneſs!" Sermon preached before the Incorporated Society for the propagation of the goſpel, &c. by the learned Dr. Newton, lord biſhop of Briſtol, 1769.

reaſon-

reaſonable, *unjuſt*, and CONTRA NATURAM *: ſo are the modern notions of Slavery, and therefore *abſolutely unlawful*, as being repugnant to the principles of the common law †.

The event has ſhewn the truth of this remark; for the common law, and the ancient profeſſors of it (as I have before obſerved) have been chiefly inſtrumental in aboliſhing Villenage ‡—Therefore, another *ſuch ſtate of ſervitude* cannot juſtly take its place, *let the ſimilarity be what it will*, becauſe the inconvenience *and injuſtice*

* Eſt quidem ſervitus *libertati contrarium*; item conſtitutio quædam de jure gentium, quâ quis *domino alieno* CONTRA NATURAM *ſubjicitur*, &c. Fleta, 2d. edit. p. 1.——The quotation here mentioned as taken from Fleta, is really a maxim of the Civil Law in theſe words: "Servitus eſt conſtitutio juris gentium, qua "quis *dominio* alieno CONTRA NATURAM ſubjicitur." Inſtit. lib. i. tit. iii. leg. 2.

† La quele condicion (la condition des villeyns) *fuit chaungé hors de fraunchiſe jeſques en ſervage* en antiquité par conſtitution de gentz NEMY PAR LE LEY DE NATURE, &c. Britton, 2d edit. p. 77.

‡ Mr. Dalrymple, in his Hiſtory of Feudal Property, fol. 74. ſpeaking of the Military Syſtem, ("once ſo univerſal and ſo ſevere") that it is now limited in the nature of its tenures, and more ſo in the perquiſites of them, obſerves thereupon, that "the people BY THEIR "CUSTOMS, and by changing many of the military "into civil feuds, effected the one; the judges BY "THEIR INTERPRETATION, and bending that inter-"pretation to the genius of the times, effected the "other."

of the former was the occasion of its annihilation, according to that excellent maxim in *common law*, " MALUS USUS ABOLEN-" DUS EST." Littleton, 2 Inst. ch. ii. p. 141. on which the great Sir Edward Cook remarks, that " *every use is evil, that is* " AGAINST REASON. Quia in consuetu-" dinibus non diuturnitas temporis, sed so-" LIDITAS RATIONIS est consideranda."

Nay, even a claim to the *mere service* of a man, *without his previous consent, or voluntary contract, is equally* UNREASONABLE and UNJUST, (though not so shocking to humanity) as the absurd claim of an *absolute property* in the person of a man.

Yet some learned men who freely and confidently condemn all pretensions to the latter, do, nevertheless, seem inclined to admit the former. Even that excellent commentator, Mr. Blackstone, though he acknowleges, b. i. c. xiv. p. 424. that " *the law* " *will protect him*" (that is a Slave or Negro) " *in the enjoyment of his person, and his pro-* " *perty. Yet,*" (says he) " *with regard to any* " *right which the master may have acquired* " *to the perpetual service of John or Thomas,* " *this will remain exactly in the same state as* " *before: for this is no more than the same* " *state of subjection for life, which every ap-* " *prentice*

" *prentice submits to for the space of seven* " *years, or sometimes for a longer term.*— " Hence too it follows, that the infamous " and unchristian practice of withholding " baptism from Negro servants, lest they " should thereby gain their liberty, is to- " tally without foundation, as well as " without excuse. The law of England " acts upon general and extensive princi- " ples: it gives liberty, rightly under- " stood, that is, protection, to a Jew, a " Turk, or a Heathen, as well as to those " who profess the true religion of Christ; " and it will not dissolve a civil obligation " between master and servant, on account " of the alteration of faith in either of the " parties: but the Slave is entitled to the " same protection in England before, as " after, baptism; and *whatever service the* " *Heathen Negro owed to his American mas-* " *ter, the same is he* BOUND TO RENDER, " *when brought to England and made a* " *Christian.*"—But by what law is the Negro " BOUND TO RENDER" such service?— This has never been declared, neither can such a law be produced, except in the case of a *written contract.*

Nevertheless, in justice to Mr. Blackstone, it must be remarked, that he hath not

not peremptorily ſaid, that the maſter *hath acquired* any right to the perpetual ſervice of John or Thomas, or that the Heathen Negro *really doth owe* ſuch ſervice to his American maſter; he only ſpeaks "*with* "*regard to any right which the maſter* MAY "have acquired,"—and of—" WHAT-" EVER SERVICE *the Heathen Negro* OWED," &c. as much as to ſay,—IF *he did owe ſuch ſervice*, the obligation is not diſſolved by his coming to England, and turning Chriſtian. And this I readily allow; for if a Negro *really owed ſervice* to his maſter, the ſame muſt certainly be *due*. Therefore, it is neceſſary to be obſerved, that when I oppoſe the claims of *perpetual ſervice*, which, to the diſgrace of this kingdom, have too frequently been made of late, I do not contradict any aſſertion of this learned gentleman; becauſe I ſpeak only of that ſervice which is NOT *due or owing*: as for inſtance, when maſters claim a *right* to the *perpetual ſervice* of a man, without being able to produce an authentic written *contract*; for, without a voluntary *contract*, there *cannot be* ANY RIGHT.

Therefore, "*with regard to* ANY RIGHT" (I mean any other right than that by con-

tract) " *which the master may have* ACQUI-
" RED *to the perpetual service of John or*
" *Thomas*," let us trace it back to its source, and examine the original means of such ACQUISITION, that we may judge how far it ought to be admitted.

" It is evident, that the Europeans, in
" sending ships yearly to the coast of Afri-
" ca, to buy slaves, without enquiring how
" those they purchase them of came by
" them, do encourage those thieves" (the Negro tyrants and plagiaries) " and tempt
" them to make a practice and trade of
" stealing their own countrymen; for this
" is the same thing in effect, as if they
" were to tell them in so many words, " *do*
" *you get men ready for us how you can,*
" *and we will take them off your hands.*"
" Besides, those men merchants not only
" encourage others in this cruel flagitious
" practice of man-stealing, but are really
" guilty of it themselves.—You will ob-
" serve, that what is done by their com-
" mand, and according to their order, I
" consider as done by themselves *. As
" those poor miserable creatures were stolen,

* " Qui per alium facit, per seipsum facere videtur." Noy's Maxims, p. 17.

" those

" thoſe who did ſteal them, *could not con-*
" *vey* ANY RIGHT *in them to others*, though
" theſe others ſhould give ever ſo much in
" purchaſe of them, any more than if they
" had them for nothing.—For thoſe pur-
" chaſers then to deprive them of their li-
" berty, and, by force, keep them in
" poſſeſſion, in whom they have *no right*,
" (ſuppoſing one man could be the pro-
" perty of another) and who never injured
" them in the leaſt, nor forfeited their
" liberty; to keep them in bonds, and
" carry them away captives, is, properly
" ſpeaking, man-ſtealing. And what ag-
" gravates this crime in the European man
" merchants, and renders it much more
" heinous in them, than in the Africans,
" is, that the former enjoy the light of the
" goſpel, and profeſs themſelves to be
" Chriſtians." (See a ſhort account of that part of Africa, inhabited by the Negroes, &c. 3d edit. p. 42.)

But to return to the author whoſe opinion I was juſt before conſidering. Though I have attempted to prevent any unjuſt concluſion, which Slaveholders and intereſted perſons might be liable to draw from ſome particular paſſages of his book, yet I muſt acknowledge, that the learned author

thor has himſelf done this already, and much more effectually. For in pages 423 and 424, he has delivered a ſovereign antidote againſt the abſurdity of ſuppoſing "ANY RIGHT *which the maſter may have* "*acquired to the perpetual ſervice of*" A MAN, except it is "*only meant of contracts to ſerve* "*or work for another.*"

It may be ſaid, indeed, that he is ſpeaking only of "*pure and proper ſlavery,*" *ſuch* (as he explains himſelf) "*whereby an abſo-* "*lute and unlimited power* * *is given to the* "*maſter over the life and fortune of the Slave.*" But his excellent arguments, which confute all pretenſions to ſuch an abſolute power, effectually invalidate at the ſame time, *the leaſt claim of ſervitude derived therefrom.* And I am convinced that the *literal force* of theſe arguments (whatſoever the private ſentiments of the author may be with reſpect to a limited ſervitude) cannot be ſet aſide by any future conſiderations.

"The three origins of the right of Sla- "very, aſſigned by Juſtinian, are all of "them built upon falſe foundations. As,

* "And indeed (ſays he) it is repugnant to reaſon "and the principles of natural law, that ſuch a ſtate "ſhould ſubſiſt any where." Id. p. 423.

"firſt,

" firſt, Slavery is held to ariſe "*jure gen-* " *tium*," from a ſtate of captivity in war; " whence Slaves are called *mancipia, quaſi* " *manu capti*. The conqueror, ſay the " civilians, had a right to the life of his " captive; and, having ſpared that, has a " right to deal with him as he pleaſes. " But it is an untrue poſition, when taken " generally, that, by the law of nature or " nations, a man may kill his enemy: he " has only a right to kill him, in particular " caſes; in caſes of abſolute neceſſity, for " ſelf-defence; and it is plain this abſolute " neceſſity did not ſubſiſt, ſince the victor " did not actually kill him, but made him " priſoner. War is itſelf juſtifiable only " on principles of ſelf-preſervation; and " therefore it gives no other right over " priſoners, but merely to diſable them " from doing harm to us, by confining " their perſons: much leſs can it give a " right to kill, torture, abuſe, plunder, or " even to enſlave an enemy, when the war " is over. Since therefore the right of " *making* Slaves by captivity, depends on " a ſuppoſed right of ſlaughter, that foun- " dation failing, the conſequence drawn " from it muſt fail likewiſe. But ſecondly,

" it

" it is ſaid, that Slavery may begin "*jure* " *civili*;" when one man ſells himſelf to " another. This, if only meant of con- " tracts to ſerve or work for another, is " very juſt: but when applied to ſtrict " Slavery, in the ſenſe of the laws of old " Rome, or modern Barbary, is alſo im- " poſſible. Every ſale implies a price, a *quid* " *pro quo*, an equivalent given to the ſeller " in lieu of what he transfers to the buyer: " but what equivalent can be given for " life and liberty, both of which (in ab- " ſolute Slavery) are held to be in the " maſter's diſpoſal?—His property alſo, " the very price he ſeems to receive, de- " volves *ipſo facto* to his maſter, the in- " ſtant he becomes his Slave. In this caſe " therefore the buyer gives nothing, and " the ſeller receives nothing: of what va- " lidity then can a ſale be, which deſtroys " the very principles upon which all ſales " are founded?—Laſtly, we are told, that " beſides theſe two ways by which Slaves " "*fiunt*," or are acquired, they may alſo be " hereditary: "*ſervi naſcuntur*;" the chil- " dren of acquired Slaves are, *jure naturæ*, " by a negative kind of birth-right, Slaves " alſo. But, this being built on the two for-

" mer

"mer rights, muſt fall together with them. "If neither captivity, nor the ſale of one's "ſelf, can by THE LAW OF NATURE AND "REASON reduce the parent to Slavery, "much leſs can they reduce the offspring. "*Upon theſe principles* THE LAW OF ENG-"LAND *abhors, and will not endure the "exiſtence of Slavery within this nation:* "ſo that when an attempt was made to "introduce it, by ſtatute 1 Edward VI. "c. 3. which ordained, that all idle vaga-"bonds ſhould be made Slaves *, and fed "upon bread, water, or ſmall drink, and "refuſe meat; ſhould wear a ring of iron "round their necks, arms, or legs; and "ſhould be compelled by beating, chain-"ing, or otherwiſe, to perform the work "aſſigned them, were it never ſo vile; "*the ſpirit of the nation could not brook this*

* The honourable Mr. juſtice Barrington, in p. 282, refers to this act to prove, that "the term of *Slave* is "certainly not unknown in our law;" as if he intended thereby to inſinuate ſomething in favour of his own doctrine, that "a Slave may continue in a ſtate of ſer-"vitude, *though he breathes the air of this* land of liber-"ty," &c. And he certainly would have been right, had not the ſaid act been ſo ſpeedily repealed. But as it was thus repealed, the recital of it is ſo far from proving any thing in favour of Slavery, that it immediately reminds us of Mr. Blackſtone's juſt remark to the contrary, that "*the ſpirit of the nation could not "brook this condition,*" &c.

"*con-*

" *condition*, even in the moſt abandoned " rogues; and therefore this ſtatute was " repealed in two years afterwards *." If theſe ſenſible and juſt arguments be duly weighed and conſidered, (whatſoever the worthy author's opinion may be in other reſpects, yet) there will be no room left for the leaſt reſervation or plea of " ANY RIGHT " which the maſter may have ACQUIR- " ED to the perpetual ſervice of John or " Thomas."

For whether the planter or merchant " *may have acquired*" this ſuppoſed *right* by purchaſe, inheritance, nativity of children from parents † in bondage, or any *other means whatſoever*, yet, as the original commencement of the bondage was manifeſtly impious and unjuſt, ſo muſt the *leaſt claim of ſervitude* upon the ſame foundation ‡, and *in this ſenſe, only*, can ſuch a right be ſaid to " *remain exactly in the ſame ſtate as* " *before*;" becauſe " *quod ab initio non va-*

* Commentaries on the Laws of England, by W. Blackſtone, Eſq; 3d edit. vol. i. b. i. ch. xiv. p. 423, 424.

† " If neither captivity nor the ſale of one's ſelf can " by the law of nature and reaſon reduce the parent to " Slavery, much leſs can they reduce the offspring."

‡ " *Debile fundamentum fallit opus.*" Noy's Maxims, p. 5.

" *let, in tractu temporis non convalescit.*" (Noy's Maxims, p. 4.)

So that the *derived* * *power or right* of the last master who detains the Slave, is certainly as unjust (with respect to the Slave himself) as the unmerciful usurpation of the first possessor.

The right which some masters have ACQUIRED to the service likewise *of Indian Slaves and their posterity*, (if any still remain in the islands) is not less unjust than the bondage of the Negroes. See an account of the European settlements in America, 2d Vol. p. 86.—The author is relating the number of inhabitants at Barbadoes, in 1650, and the proportion of *Blacks and Indian Slaves*, " the former of which " Slaves" (says he) " they bought; the " latter, they acquired by means not *at* " *all to their honour*; for they *seized upon* " those unhappy men *without any pretence*, " in the neighbouring islands, *and carried* " *them into Slavery*. A practice which has " rendered the Caribbee Indians irrecon- " cileable to us ever since."

A considerable number of Carolina Indians were also formerly reduced to the

* " *Derivativa potestas non potest esse major primitivâ.*" Id. p. 3.

Engliſh bondage in the Weſt Indies,—and the *acquired right* of the perſons who were the firſt proprietors of them, was equally unjuſt and diſhonourable.

The occaſion and commencement of this wretched captivity was as follows:

" *The Sewees*, a particular tribe of In-
" dians in Carolina, ſeeing ſeveral ſhips
" coming in, to bring the Engliſh ſupplies
" from Old England, one chief part of
" their cargo being for trade with the In-
" dians, ſome of the craftieſt of them had
" obſerved, that the ſhips came always in
" at one place; which made them very
" confident, that way was the exact road
" to England; and ſeeing ſo many ſhips
" come from thence, they believed it
" could not be far thither, eſteeming the
" Engliſh that were among them, no bet-
" ter than cheats, and thought, if they
" could carry the ſkins and furrs they got
" themſelves to England, which was in-
" habited by a better ſort of people than
" thoſe ſent amongſt them, that then they
" ſhould purchaſe twenty times the value
" for every pelt they ſold abroad, in con-
" ſideration of what rates they ſold for at
" home.

" The intended barter was exceeding " well approved of, and after a general " confultation of the ableft heads amongft " them, it was, nemine contradicente, " agreed upon, immediately to make an " addition of their fleet, by building more " canoes, and thofe to be of the beft fort, " and biggeft fize, as fit for their intended " difcovery.—Some Indians were employ" ed about making the canoes, others to " hunting, every one to the poft he was " moft fit for, all endeavours tending to" wards an able fleet and cargo for Eu" rope.

" The affair was carried on with a great " deal of fecrecy and expedition, fo as in " a fmall time they had gotten a navy, " loading, provifions, and hands ready to " fail; leaving only the old, impotent and " minors at home, till their fuccefsful re" turn.

" The wind prefenting, they fet up " their mat fails, and were fcarce out of " fight, when there rofe a tempeft, which " it is fuppofed carried one part of thefe " Indian merchants by way of the other " world, whilft the others were taken up " at fea by *an Englifh fhip, and fold for*

" *Slaves*

" *Slaves to the islands.*" (Hist. of Carolina, by James Lawson, Gent. Surveyor General of North Carolina, p. 11.)

The ignorance and simplicity of these poor uncultivated Heathens, surely can never be alledged as a sufficient warrant to justify this uncharitable and base act of *the more Heathenish English!*

There is no accounting for such extreme hardness of heart in our countrymen on board the English ship; unless it may be esteemed one of the dire effects of the antichristian toleration of Slavery in our colonies, which (we may presume) was become so familiar to these unworthy Englishmen, as to have entirely debauched their former principles of humanity and brotherly love.

What depravity, therefore, and corruption of manners have we not reason to dread, if a state of bondage is likewise admitted even into old England itself!

If there be any thing due, as of right, from either of the parties (master or Slave) on their arrival in England, the debt must certainly be on the master's side, on account of the Slave's former services.

The ſcanty allowance of food and cloaths (uſually given to the Slave during his ſervitude) cannot be conſidered as a ſufficient acknowledgment for the above, becauſe theſe were not given for the ſake of the Slave, but merely for *the intereſt of the maſter*, * to enable the former to continue his daily labour; ſo that it muſt be conſidered much in the ſame light, as the foddering of a horſe, or the expence of *fattening cattle for ſlaughter*; becauſe the food is not given on any other conſideration, than for the profit of the owner.

Let the planter or merchant, therefore, " *diligently* conſider, whether there will

* " I confeſs, as to the proviſion for their bodies, " (ſays the Rev. Mr. Godwyn in " the Negroes and " Indians Advocate," p. 81.) they deny it not to be " expedient, or fit to be allowed them: but this, not " as their *right* or *due*, but as conducive to the *maſter's* " *convenience and profit*, THE MOST OPERATIVE AND " UNIVERSALLY OWNED PRINCIPLE OF THIS PLACE, " *and indeed of* THE WHOLE PLANTATIONS. They " conſider it only in order to the enabling their people " to undergo their *labour*, without which themſelves " cannot get riches and great eſtates; but nothing (ſo " far as I could ever learn) for the wretches *health* and " preſervation. And both their diſcourſe and moſt " current practice, do declare no leſs; in neither of " which doth appear much *tenderneſs*. Pity to huma- " nity being here reputed a *puſillanimous* weakneſs, " and a very back friend to intereſt. Whence their " houſes are ſo plentifully ſtored with tormenting *en-* " *gines*, and devices to execute their *cruelty*, &c."

" not

" not always *remain to the Slave* a ſuperior " property, or right, *to the fruit of his own* " *labour*; and more eſpecially, *to his own* " *perſon*, that Being which was given him " by God, and which none but the giver " can juſtly claim?" (See ſhort account of the Slave Trade, &c. 3d edit. in the Concluſion of the Editor, p. 42.)

" *The law favoureth a man's perſon before* " *his poſſeſſions*," (Noy's Maxims, p. 6 & 7.) that a man's property in *his own perſon*, is certainly far ſuperior, and ought to be preferred to any claim whatſoever, that another perſon can poſſibly have upon him, on account of his having been formerly a Slave, private property, *poſſeſſion* or *mere chattel*.—If this, on examination, is really found to be true, the maſter is ſo far from having " acquired" any " right" by former *poſſeſſion* to the " *perpetual ſervice of John* " *or Thomas*," that he is, himſelf, *become a debtor* to his quondam Slaves for all the involuntary ſervices, for which the latter have never been paid; and therefore the former is certainly bound in ſtrict juſtice and honour, (though not perhaps in law) to make ample amends to their poor injured Slaves for the ſame; " *not only as an act*

" *of justice* to the individuals, but as a debt " due, on account of the oppression and in- " justice perpetrated on them or their an- " cestors; and as the best means to avert " the judgments of God, which it is to " be feared will fall on families and coun- " tries, in proportion as they have, more " or less, defiled themselves with this ini- " quitous traffick." (Short account of the Slave Trade, &c. p. 65.)

Because even when the Slave was in the plantation he *owed* no service to the master, as really due *of right* from himself—He submitted, indeed, to his master, while he thought himself under a necessity of doing so, through fear of that undue authority of the master, which the tyrannical and unchristian laws of our West India colonies enforce.

But as soon as he was removed out of the reach of those irreligious * laws, *all obligation to service ceased,* together with

* On a late trial in Westminster-hall, (at which the author was present) it appeared from the information of a West Indian gentleman, that the intercourse which the planters allow between their male and female Slaves, is generally no more than what the ancients called a Contubernium, and that they " *look upon marriage to be* " *rather unlawful for their Slaves.*"

Also that their laws *do not punish the murder of a Negro Slave* any further, than that the murderer is liable to

pay

the unjuſt authority of the maſter, who no longer has any power to compel his quondam Slave to ſerve him; for if any compulſion ſhould be uſed for that purpoſe in England, (or perhaps in moſt parts of Europe *) the ſame muſt be at the maſter's peril; becauſe even the advocates for this " *perpetual ſervice*" are obliged to allow (as I have before obſerved) that " *the law will* " *protect him*" (the Slave) " *in the enjoyment* " *of his perſon and his property.*"

For though a poor Slave from the Eaſt or Weſt Indies, may not have been " thought " of by the legiſlature, or had in contemplation," (that is with reſpect to his parti-

pay the ſmall fine of 25*l.* and (if the Slave is not his own) the cuſtomary price at which the Slave is rated. So that the epithet " *irreligious*," (as it admits of varirious degrees of ſignification) is too mild a term to be applied to ſome of the plantation laws and cuſtoms, becauſe theſe in particular which I have mentioned, are certainly *irreligious* to ſuch an extreme degree, that they ought rather to be called *diabolical*, or by any other epithet, which is capable of expreſſing *the moſt conſummate wickedneſs*.—It is ſurely the plaineſt indication of a moſt abandoned and profligate generation, that their laws and cuſtoms ſhould be found directly repugnant to the laws of God; for it is a maxim in law, that " *the inferior* " *law muſt give place to the ſuperior, man's laws to God's* " *laws.*" Noy's Maxims, p. 19.

* " Slaves may claim their freedom as ſoon as they " come into England, Germany, France, &c." Groenwig. Vinnius. ad. ht. quoted in Wood's C. Inſt. b. 1. c. ii. p. 114.

cular

cular ſtate or condition, as an Indian, Mulatto, Negro or Slave,) when the ſeveral ſtatutes againſt oppreſſion were made; yet with reſpect to his condition *as a man*, he is certainly included; becauſe, in this capacity, he cannot be conſidered in law, as "*a thing newly created*," and therefore not thought of by the legiſlature,—"*For no* "*man*, of what *eſtate or condition that he be*, "*ſhall be put* out of land or tenement, nor "taken, nor impriſoned, &c. without be- "ing brought in anſwer by due proceſs of "the law," *—becauſe, "*every man may* "*be free to ſue for and defend his right in* "*our courts, and elſewhere, according to* "*law*." † The ſame is to be obſerved likewiſe with reſpect to the general capacity of Negroes as SUBJECTS, when in England, for as "EVERY ALIEN AND STRANGER "*born out of the King's obeiſance, not being* "*denizen, which now or hereafter ſhall come* "*in or to this realm*, &c. IS BOUNDEN *by* "*and unto the laws and ſtatutes of this realm*, "*and to all and ſingular the contents of the* "*ſame*," ‡ ſo it follows of courſe, that a Negro or Indian Slave in this *general capa-*

* 28 Edward III. c. iii.

† 20 Edward, c. iv.

‡ 32 Hen. VIII. c. xvi. ſect. 9. p. 511.

city

city of alien, muſt be *accounted a ſubject*, while he is reſiant in this kingdom; and, as ſuch, he muſt neceſſarily be protected by the Habeas Corpus act, || notwithſtanding that his *particular ſtate or condition of Slave, Negro, or Indian*, might not have "*been conſidered or had in contemplation*," when the ſaid act was made; becauſe "NO "SUBJECT *of this realm, that now is or* "*hereafter ſhall be an inhabitant*, &c.— "*ſhall or may be ſent priſoner*," &c. and becauſe the act is expreſly intended "*for the* "*better ſecuring* THE LIBERTY OF THE "SUBJECT." For ſuppoſe any perſon ſhould preſume to ſay, that the French proteſtant Refugees, for inſtance, (though they are as good and as loyal ſubjects as any in his Majeſty's dominions) are not entitled to the privileges and protection of the Habeas Corpus act, or of any of the other acts recited above, becauſe they were

|| This act, as well as the other three acts laſt mentioned, are ſo frequently quoted and commented upon, in the foregoing parts of this work, that the author is apprehenſive, he may be blamed for tautology; nevertheleſs, as the genuine ſenſe of theſe ſeveral acts is of the utmoſt importance to the preſent ſubject, he was rather willing to run the riſk of offending by repetition, than to ſeem at all backward or deficient in enforcing ſuch material points.

not

not eſtabliſhed in England, when the ſaid acts were made, and therefore could not have been "*conſidered or had in contempla-*" *tion by the legiſlature,*" ſo as to be included therein.

If ſuch an argument, I ſay, ſhould ever be advanced, I doubt not, but that every ſenſible man of the law would moſt readily join with me in condemning the doctrine as impious, and contrary to the meaning of our laws; and yet theſe ſame alien ſubjects, *or even the gentlemen of the law themſelves,* though Engliſhmen born, are not protected by any other interpretation of the ſaid laws, than that to which the Negroes and Indians who live in England, *are equally intitled*; (viz. the conſideration of their *general capacity* as MEN and SUBJECTS, according to *the letter* of the above-mentioned ſtatutes,) for they are not at all conſidered in their *particular capacities* of French Proteſtant Refugee, Lawyer, or by any other particular denomination or profeſſion whatſoever.—Wherefore we may ſafely conclude THAT ALL SUBJECTS, both natural born and alien, of every denomination, (without exception, *real or implied)* muſt neceſſarily be protected according to the literal meaning,

and

and unavoidable conſtruction of the Habeas Corpus act. For there is no law, nor no exceptions (whether real or *implied,)* to juſtify a breach of what is there enacted, excepting the particular caſes mentioned in the 13th and 14th ſections; as for inſtance, ſect. xiii.—"Provided always, that nothing "in this act *extend to give benefit to any* "*perſon,* who ſhall by contract in writing "agree with any merchant," &c.—So the 14th ſection allows *the tranſportation* of "perſons lawfully convicted of any felony," who "ſhall, in open court, *pray to be tranſ*-"*ported,*" &c.——"*this act, or any thing* "*therein contained, notwithſtanding.*"

Therefore it muſt neceſſarily be "*im*-"*plied,*" that the general terms of this act "*extend to give benefit,*" in all other caſes whatſoever, which can fairly be ſaid to come within the letter of it; and every attempt to *detain, impriſon,* or TRANSPORT any perſon whatſoever as a Slave, while he is an inhabitant of this kingdom, muſt inevitably be conſtrued as an offence againſt this ſtatute, becauſe every individual muſt certainly be conſidered within the letter and meaning of it, with reſpect to his *general capacity of* SUBJECT, whether *he be*

native

native or alien, white or negro; and muſt be protected by it accordingly. No reaſonable man (I think) will accuſe me of ſtraining the letter of the law to a ſiniſter purpoſe; for the conſtruction here laid down is founded upon the generous principle * of our laws, and cannot be rejected without a manifeſt perverſion both of *the letter* and *meaning* of the act.

A Slave therefore, on his coming to England, muſt be abſolutely *free*, and not ſubject to any "claims whatſoever of *perpetual* "*ſervice*," on account of his former Slavery, as ſome have imagined: becauſe the doctrine of "*a perpetual ſervice due to the* "*maſter*," *is*, in effect, *a vaſſalage*, and, as ſuch, is inconſiſtent with the preſent ſpirit of our laws.——For when it was thought proper, as well as equitable, to

* "The law favours liberty, and the freedom of a "man from impriſonment, and therefore kind interpre-"tations ſhall be made on its behalf." Wood 'sInſt. c. i. p. 25. For human nature requireth favour in the cauſe of freedom, more than in other circumſtances.—"Humana natura, in libertatis cauſa, favorem ſemper "magis quam in cauſis aliis deprecetur." Forteſcue, c. xlvii. p. 109. v.

In caſes of doubt, ſays the civil law, the cauſe of liberty is to take place. "*Quoties dubia interpretatio* "*libertatis eſt, ſecundum libertatem reſpondendum.*" Digeſt. lib. l. tit. xvii. leg. 20. and again leg. 122. "*Liber-*"*tas omnibus rebus favorabilior eſt.*"

abolish

abolish the *vassalage of Scotland,* (which unnatural yoke of bondage was justly esteemed " *dangerous to the community* *,") the most effectual means for this salutary purpose were, " *to extend the influ-" ence, benefit, and protection of the King's laws*" (that is, the laws of England) " *and " courts of justice to all his Majesty's sub-" jects in Scotland* †.—This is a plain proof that the laws of England were esteemed obnoxious to any involuntary bondage without a just cause, and to all private jurisdiction whatsoever; so that *an extension* of the " *influence, benefit, and protection*" *of these laws* was considered as a relief to our fellow-subjects in Scotland, from all private oppression.

There are, however, some local exceptions (in the 20th and 21st sections) to this extension of English liberty, which, for the sake of humanity and justice, as

* " The statute of the present King (then George " II.) came last, which abolished some, and limited " others, of such of the territorial jurisdictions as were " found *dangerous to the community*, &c." Dalrymple's History of Feudal Property, p. 246.

† See act of 20 Geo. II. intituled " An act for taking away and abolishing the heretable jurisdictions " in that part of Great Britain called Scotland, &c."

well

well as for the honour of the kingdom of Scotland, I ſincerely wiſh to ſee expunged.

Nevertheleſs we ought thankfully to remember, that in every other place of Great Britain, where thoſe exceptions do not bind, all private juriſdiction or "*acquired* "*right of perpetual ſervice,*" muſt neceſſarily be conſidered as null and void by the "*influence, benefit and protection of the King's* "*laws and courts of juſtice,*" according to the true tenor and meaning of the ſaid act with reſpect to Scotland; and according to the ſenſe of the legiſlature, at that time, with reſpect to England.

What right, therefore, can a maſter "*ac*"*quire*" by his former tyranny in the Weſt Indies, "*to the perpetual ſervice of John or* "*Thomas*" when in England? and how can ſuch a *right* (except a written contract can be produced) be ſuppoſed to remain "*exactly* "*in the ſame ſtate as before?*"

The laws of England admit of no ſuch right, and therefore cannot enforce it, and with reſpect to the plantation laws, I hope no one will preſume to inſinuate that their influence can extend in the leaſt degree to the mother country, howſoever they may have been confirmed for the uſe of the colonies; for

for "*ſhould the attempt be made to import any* "*ſtrange laws, contrary* TO THE FUNDA-" MENTAL MAXIMS *of our own, it would*" (I hope) "*always be repulſed with that in-*" *dignation it ſo juſtly deſerves.*" Dr. Bever's Diſcourſe on Juriſprudence and the Civil Law.

Whatſoever regard, therefore, may, or ought to be paid to the plantation laws at Weſtminſter, in ſome particular caſes when the queſtion of *property* relates to Slaves remaining in the colony where thoſe laws were made; yet when the Negro Slave is once removed to England, he cannot in the leaſt be affected by any other laws than thoſe of England, and muſt neceſſarily be protected by *the common law of England*, as well as by the penal ſtatutes in the ſame manner, and as effectually, as any other alien ſubject whatſoever, which I hope is already ſufficiently demonſtrated.

The honourable Mr. juſtice Barrington (in his obſervations on the more ancient ſtatutes, p. 280.) mentions a notion originally inculcated by Wycliff and his followers, which began to prevail ſo early as the time of that great lawyer Fitzherbert, "OF " ITS BEING CONTRARY TO THE PRINCI-

"PLES OF THE CHRISTIAN RELIGION, "THAT ANY ONE SHOULD BE A SLAVE," and from hence, (ſays he) "in more mo- "dern times, Slavery hath been ſuppoſed to "be *inconſiſtent with the common law*, which "is ſaid to be founded on Chriſtianity. Be "the law as it may, the perſuaſion contri- "buted greatly to the aboliſhing Villen- "age; and the principle, whether adopted "by *the common law* from Chriſtianity, or "otherwiſe, cannot be too much com- "mended or inſiſted upon:" Yet he is pleaſed to add,—"*I cannot, however, but* "*think*" (ſays he) "*that neither the Chriſtian* "*religion, nor the common law, ever inculcat-* "*ed or eſtabliſhed ſuch a tenet*." Now, with reſpect to the former, the iniquitous and in-human practices introduced into the American colonies, by the toleration of Slavery in thoſe parts are ſufficient proofs, that Slavery is deſtructive of *morality* and *charity*, and cannot therefore be *conſiſtent* with the Chriſtian religion; becauſe it gives worldly minded men a power to deprive their Slaves of inſtruction and ſpiritual improvement, by continually oppreſſing them with labour. For mankind in general, howſoever religious they may eſteem themſelves, are not ſo perfect as to be ſafely intruſted with abſolute power. Avarice, choler, luſt, revenge, caprice, and all other human infirmities, according to the different diſpoſitions of men, will too frequently *enſlave* the maſter himſelf, ſo as to render him intirely unfit to be entruſted with an abſolute power over others. "THAT ANY "ONE SHOULD BE A SLAVE," muſt therefore be contrary to the law *of nature and reaſon*, and conſequently "*is inconſiſtent with* "*the common law*": ſo that the opinion of the great Fitzherbert is certainly better founded, than that of the honourable and learned gentleman who diſſents from him in this particular. And I hope I have before ſufficiently proved, that *the common law* and the ancient profeſſors of it, after a long conflict with the barbarity of ſeveral generations, were the principal means of aboliſhing the Engliſh Slavery.

I muſt alſo obſerve, that "*the perpetual* "*ſervice*" of a ſlave cannot, with propriety, be compared to the temporary ſervice of an apprentice *, becauſe the latter is due only in conſequence of *a voluntary contract*,

* See Commentaries on the Laws of England, by William Blackſtone, Eſq; Vol. I. ch. xiv. p. 425.

wherein both parties have a mutual advantage; but in the former caſe, there *is no contract*, neither can a contract be even IMPLIED, becauſe *the free conſent of both parties* cannot poſſibly be IMPLIED likewiſe; and, without this, every kind of contract (in the very nature and Idea of ſuch an obligation) is abſolutely *null and void.*—For even a written contract would be uſeleſs, as I have before obſerved, unleſs the maſter could prove, that he had previouſly granted his Slave a manumiſſion in the colonies, and that the quondam Slave *was abſolutely free*, when he entered into the ſaid contract, otherwiſe the Slave may fairly *plead compulſion and dureſs* *, which muſt inevitably render the *contract illegal*; becauſe, " *perſons under ſome illegal reſtraint,* " *or force, as dureſs, man'eſs,*" (ſee Sir Matthew Hale's Analyſis, ſect. i. p. 4.) " come " under the title of non-ability," for with reſpect to their capacity of *taking or diſpoſing*, they are in law *diſabled.*—So that as

* " If one is under a juſt fear of being impriſoned, " beaten, &c. and he ſeals a bond to him that menaces " him, it is *dureſs per minas*, and in both caſes he may " *plead the dureſs and avoid the action.*" Wood's Inſtit. b. i. c. i. p. 25.

See alſo Baron Puffendorf, (quoted in p. 10.) in the firſt part of this work.

a real

a real contract *, made under the reftraint

* A learned friend has favoured me with the following remarks, fhewing how this matter is confidered in the Civil Law.

Before *any contract* can be valid, the civil law requires three conditions, (among many others) which are effential and indifpenfible.

1. That the parties contracting fhould have a *legal capacity*; but a Slave does not come under this defcription; for " quod attinet ad jus civile, fervi pro nullis " habentur:" and again, " fervitutem mortalitati fere " comparamus." Digeft. lib. l. tit. xvii. leg. 32 and 209. A Slave therefore has no more civil or legal capacity, than a man that is actually dead.

2. They muft have an *intention* to contract. " In ea " quæ ex duorum pluriumve confenfu agitur, omnium " *voluntas* fpectetur." Digeft. xliv. vii. 31. and again, " in conventionibus *contrahentium voluntatem*, potius " quam verba fpectari placuit." Digeft. l. xvi. 219. Now it can hardly be fuppofed, that any one can intend to confent to any contract that fhall deprive him of the common rights of *humanity*.

3. They muft have *liberty*; when therefore the free exercife of that is obftructed by force or fear, the act done in confequence thereof is void, for " nil *confenfui* " tam contrarium eft quam *vis atque metus*, quem com- " probare contra bonos mores eft." Digeft. l. xvii. 116. At the fame time however, to obviate frivolous pretences, the law fays, " vani timoris jufta excufatio non " eft." Digeft. l. xvii. 184. and to fhew what fhall be confidered as a juft force or fear, defcribes them in the following manner: " vis eft majoris rei impetus, qui " repelli non poteft; and again, " non vani hominis, " fed qui merito in hominem conftantiffimum cadat." Digeft. iv. ii. 2, 5, and 6. A Slave, either captive in war, or fold into bondage, not being under the protection of law, is intirely deprived of all liberty of acting, and may be juftly faid to be *under fear* of any punifhment, however cruel, that his arbitrary mafter may pleafe to inflict upon him, and *cannot* therefore be a party *to any contract*, whether *exprefs* or *implied*.

of

of imprisonment or Slavery, cannot be valid, it is very evident, that the notion of "A CONTRACT IMPLIED," (when under the like circumstances,) must be entirely without foundation.

Hence the idea of "*a perpetual service*" due to the master, without the free consent of the servant, is certainly inconsistent with the fundamental maxims of the English law, and cannot, with justice, be compared to the *temporary service of an apprentice.*

I hope I may now safely conclude, without further contradiction, that the opinion of Lord Chief Justice Holt, concerning Negroes, is indisputably right; viz. "*as soon as a Negro comes into England, he becomes free*:" that is, *absolutely free*, without being subject to any *foreign claims* of service whatsoever; for "it is the honour "and safety, and therefore the just desire "of kingdoms that recognize no superior but God, that their laws have those "two qualifications; viz. 1st, That they "be not dependant upon any foreign "power, &c.—2dly, That they taste not "of *bondage or servitude*; for that derogates "from *the dignity* of the kingdom, and "from

" from *the liberties* of the people thereof." Sir Matthew Hale's Hiſtory of the Common Law, ch. v. p. 70.

" Shew me then the *ſphere* of man's *Be-" ing*, and you may quickly find the *mea-" ſure* of his *freedom*;" (ſays the author of a book intituled, Rights of the Kingdom, p. 140.) " his being is by all agreed " to be *Rational*; and *reaſon* therefore is " the proper meaſure of his *liberty*.—For " he is *then free*, when his *activity* is pre-" ſerved equal or proportional to his *Being*; " this is *Rational*, and ſo muſt that: and " man is then, *and then only free*, when he " can act, *what he ſhould act*, *according to " right reaſon*.—*This is the law of his na-" ture, which is rational*; and *reaſon* is his " royal collar of S. S. S. or a chain of " precious pearls, which *nature* hath put " about his neck and arms, as a badge of " honour and moſt happy freedom."

" This digreſſion would be ſcarce excu-" ſable; but that our law doth ſo adore " *right reaſon*, that (it) is a maxim, *what " is contrary to reaſon, is contrary to law*."

FINIS.

E R R A T A.

Page 13. line 7. for *as an abſolute authority*, read *as abſolute an authority.*

Page 58. line 12. for *Servants*, read *Servant.*

Page 99. line 7. for *perſon of men*, read *perſons.*

Page 147. line 7. the Sewees, a particular tribe of Indians in Carolina, " ſeeing ſeveral ſhips, &c. the quotation begins at the word " *ſeeing*, &c.

Page 149. line 2. for *James Lawſon*, read *John Lawſon.*

Page 157. line 3. for *no exceptions*, read *any exceptions.*